WALKING IN THE SPIRIT
BY

A.B. Simpson

(1843 - 1919)

482

— knowdge puff up → lake of fire.
— grafted.

Walking in the Spirit

Chapter 1: LIVING IN THE SPIRIT.

"If we live in the Spirit, let us also walk in the Spirit." Gal. 5: 25.

What is it to Live in the Spirit?

It is to be born of the Spirit. It is to have received a new spiritual life from above. "That which is born of the flesh is flesh, that which is born of the Spirit is Spirit. "Except a man be born of water and of the Spirit, he cannot enter into the Kingdom of God." "If any man be in Christ, he is a new creature; old things have passed away; behold, all things have become new." We may have the brightest intellectual life, the most unblemished moral character, and the most amiable qualities of disposition, and yet without the new life of the Holy Spirit in our heart, we can no more enter Heaven than the lovely canary that sings in our window can become a member of our family, or the gentle lamb that our children play with can sit down at our table, and share our domestic fellowship and enjoyment. It belongs to a different world, and nothing but a new nature and human heart could bring it into fellowship with our human life. The most exalted intellect, and the most attractive, natural disposition, reach no higher than the earthly. The Kingdom of Heaven consists of the family of God, those who have risen to an entirely different sphere, and received a nature as much above the intellectual and the moral as God is above an angel.

A modern writer has finely wrought out this wonderful thought of the difference between the various orders of life, even in the natural world. The little tuft of moss that grows upon the granite rock can look down from immeasurable heights upon the mass of stone on which it rests and say, "I am transcendently above you, for I have life, vegetable life, and you are an inorganic mass!" And yet, as we ascend one step, the smallest insect that crawls upon the majestic palm tree can look down upon the most beautiful production of the vegetable world and say, "I am transcendently above you, for I have animal life, and you have not even the consciousness of your own loveliness, or of the little creature that feeds upon your blossom!" Still higher we ascend, until we reach the world of mind; and the youngest child of the most illiterate peasant can say to the mightiest creations of the animal world, to the majestic lion, king of the forest; the soaring eagle of the skies; the many-tinted bird of Paradise, or the noble steed that bears his master, like the whirlwind, over the desert, "I am your lord, for I possess intellectual life, and you have neither soul nor reason, and must perish with your expiring breath, and become like the clods beneath your feet, but I shall live forever. But there is still another step beyond all this. There is a spiritual world which is as much higher than the intellectual as that is above the physical; and the humblest and most uncultured Christian, who has just learned to pray, and say, "Our Father, who art in Heaven" from the depths of a regenerate heart, is as much above the loftiest genius of the world of mind as he is above the material creation at his feet.

This is the meaning of Christianity; it is the breath of a new nature; it is the translation of the soul into a higher universe and a loftier scale of being, even introducing it into the family of God Himself and making it a part of the Divine nature. This is indeed a stupendous mystery, and a bestowment whose glory may well fill our hearts with everlasting wonder, as we cry with the adoring apostle, "Behold what manner of love the Father hath bestowed upon us, that we should be called the sons of God!"

Not by adoption merely are we thus admitted to the Father's house, but by actual birth; from the very bosom of the Holy Ghost, as from a heavenly mother, has our new spirit been born; just as literally as Jesus Christ Himself was born of the eternal Spirit in the bosom of Mary. So it might be said of every newborn soul: "The Holy Ghost shall come upon thee, and the power of the Highest shall overshadow thee; therefore, that holy thing which shall be born of thee shall be called the Son of God." Beloved, do we thus live in the Spirit? This is everlasting life.

2. To live in the Spirit is also to be baptized of the Holy Ghost, and have the Spirit as a Divine person living in us. There is something higher than the new birth, namely, the entering in of the Comforter, in His personal fullness and glory, to dwell in the consecrated heart and abide there for ever. Jesus was born of the Spirit in Bethlehem, but He was baptized of the Spirit thirty years later on the banks of the Jordan; and this made all the difference which we trace between His quiet years at Nazareth and His public ministry in Galilee and Judea. From that time there were two persons united in the ministry of Jesus of Nazareth. The Holy Ghost, as a Divine person, was united with the person of Jesus Christ, and was the source of His power and the inspiration of His teaching; and He constantly represented Himself as speaking the words and doing the works which the Spirit in Him prompted.

And so there is in the believer's life a similar experience, when the soul truly converted to God yields itself wholly to His control and becomes the living temple of the Almighty Spirit, who henceforth dwells in us, and walks in us, giving us not only a new nature, which we receive in regeneration, but a Divine Guest, a Presence to dwell in that new nature as its controlling guide and Almighty strength.

Then is fulfilled the double promise of Ezekiel: "A new heart will I give unto you and a new spirit will I put within you, and I will put my Spirit within you and will cause you to walk in my statutes, and ye shall keep my judgments and do them." Henceforth, we live in the Spirit in a higher sense than even before our conversion. Our life is not only spiritual but divine. Henceforth, it is not we who live, but Christ who liveth in us, and we draw from Him, through the Holy Ghost, every moment, life, and health, and joy, and peace. It is not living through the Spirit, but living in the Spirit. He is the very element of our new existence; before us, behind us, above us, beneath us, within us, beyond us, we are buried in Him, lost in Him, encompassed by Him as by the air we breathe. This is the yet higher mystery of the new life, greater than the new birth. This is the secret which Paul declares was hid for ages and generations, but now made manifest to His saints. "Christ in you the hope of glory."

It is, indeed, an epoch in the soul's existence as wonderful in its measure as when the Son of God became incarnate on earth, when the Holy One crosses the threshold of the heart, and makes the spirit his personal residence, sits down upon the throne of the human will and assumes the government and control of all our being and destiny. Henceforth, we may indeed walk with holy veneration and exalted hope, exultant in joy and triumph as wondering angels declare, "Behold the tabernacle of God is with men, He will dwell with them and they shall be His people; God Himself shall be with them and shall be their God."

Beloved, have you claimed this high privilege, and received this heavenly Guest into the golden casket of your regenerated souls? Have you received the invaluable jewel of the Living One Himself, as the treasure in the earthen vessel and the glory in the midst?

3. To live in the Spirit is to be sanctified by the Spirit; to receive the Spirit of holiness and thus be delivered from the power of sin. They, who thus receive the Holy Ghost can say, "The spirit of life in Christ Jesus hath made me free from the law of sin and death." This is divine holiness; it is the entrance into a sinful heart of a new life which excludes the old and takes its place. It is not the cleansing of the flesh or the improving of the life of self; but it is the imparting to us of a new life which is in itself essentially pure and cannot sin, even the holy life of God.

In our childhood many of us have roamed through the native woods and seen some old fallen forest tree rotting where it lay. Through the decaying wood the earthworms and insects burrow, and perhaps the adder has built its nest and raised its poisonous brood, so that we have feared to sit down on the old, putrefying mass, and have thought of it as a type of corruption and decay. That mass of putrefaction may well represent the ruin of our sinful nature. But have we not sometimes seen a little shoot of unsullied whiteness in the early spring growing up through the rotten wood, and rising out of the mass of corruption as undefiled as the sunny wing of a dove, or the gentle hand of a babe, beautiful and pure, and unstained even by the touch of the corrupting element around it, until it has grown into a tree and covered itself with luxurious green, and our hands have often plucked from its branches the luscious berries of the summer woods? It was life in the midst of death, purity amid corruption, having no connection whatever with the soil in which it grew and incapable of mixture with its defilement.

Precisely so is the life of holiness in the soul. Like that stainless shoot, it grew from a Divine root, and has nothing in common with our own sinful nature. It is of heavenly origin, and it grows up within us in its own Divine purity and fruitfulness, until it ripens into all the rich fruition of a consecrated and heavenly life, and yet at every stage we feel that it is in no sense our own life, but the indwelling presence and purity of God Himself.

Beloved, have we received this sanctifying Spirit and learned this heavenly secret of holy living? And in all the exquisite rest and conscious purity and overcoming power of His presence, have we learned to live in the Spirit?

4. To live in the Spirit is to receive the quickening life of the Holy Ghost in our physical being, and to find in Him the source of constant stimulus and strength for all the faculties of our mind, and all the functions of our body; "For if the Spirit of Him that raised up Jesus from the dead dwell in us, He that raised up Christ from the dead shall also quicken our mortal bodies by His Spirit, that dwelleth in us." The subtle principle of life itself came originally, no doubt, from His inbreathing at man's creation, and why should it be thought anything incredible that He should still breathe upon our flesh the quickening life of the ascended Son of God? Are we not members of His body, and His flesh, and His bones, and does He not speak of a distinct sense in which our body is the temple of the Holy Ghost? Indeed it was the Holy Ghost, who, during Christ's ministry, always gave efficiency to His healing word, and who, through the apostles, continued

to perform the same works of supernatural power. He is still the same infinite and inexhaustible life, and the bodies of His consecrated people are the subjects of His Divine influence, and His sustaining love and care.

Have we learned, beloved, the secret of His strength, and like Samson of old, do we know what it is to be moved by the Spirit until the earthen vessel becomes mighty through God to do and endure where earthly strength must fail? They, who thus "wait upon the Lord, shall renew their strength; mount up with wings as eagles; run, and not be weary, walk, and not faint."

Chapter 2: WALKING IN THE SPIRIT

I. What is it to Walk in the Spirit?

Generally, it may be said, it is to maintain the habit of dependence upon the Holy Ghost for our entire life; spirit, soul and body. We know what it is at times to enjoy His conscious presence. We live in the Spirit, we have felt the touch of His quickening life, now let us walk in the Spirit. Let us abide in this fellowship. Let us lean continually upon His strength, and drink unceasingly from His life, a babe from its mother's breast. But more particularly.

1. To walk in the Spirit is to recognize the Spirit as present and abiding in us. How often, after we have asked His presence, we treat Him as if He had deceived us, and cry to Him as if He were afar off! Let us recognize Him as having come, and address Him as a present and indwelling friend. He will always meet our recognition, and speak to us as the ancient presence, not from the mount, or the pillar of fire, but from the tabernacle, and from the holy of holies in our inmost heart.

2. It means to trust Him and count upon Him in the emergencies of life, to regard Him as one who has undertaken our cause and expects to be called upon in every time of need, and will unfailingly be found faithful and all-sufficient in every crisis. The very name Paraclete means one that we can always call upon and find at our side. We must trust the Holy Spirit, and expect Him to respond to our need as implicitly as we expect the air to answer the opening of our lungs, and the sunrise to meet us in the morning. And yet how many treat the Holy Spirit as if He were a capricious and most unreliable friend! How may of our prayers are despairing groans or scolding reflections on His love and faithfulness!

It was for this that Moses lost the Promised Land; instead of quietly speaking to the rock and expecting its waters to flow forth to meet his call, he struck it with hasty and unbelieving violence and spake as one who did not fully trust the love and faithfulness of God. There is no need that we should strike the rock, or cry, like Baal's priests to the distant heavens for help. Let us gently and implicitly claim the love that is always in advance even of our prayer. Let us speak in the whisper of childlike trust to that bosom which is ever ready to pour its fullness into our empty hearts, and lo! the waters will gush forth, and the desert of our sorrows, doubts, and fears will blossom as the rose.

3. We must consult the Holy Spirit if we would walk in the Spirit. We shall often find that the things that seem most easy will fail and disappoint us when we rely upon their apparent probability and the mere promise of outward circumstances, and we shall also find where we

commit our way unto Him, and acknowledge Him in all our ways, that He will so direct our paths that the things which seemed most difficult and improbable, will become the easiest and the most successful. He would teach us thus to trust in Him with all our heart, and lean not unto our own understanding; in all our ways to acknowledge Him and He will direct our steps.

The chief condition of His Almighty power is that we shall first have His omniscient wisdom. He is given to us as our wonderful Counselor and also as our Mighty God. And I have never taken Him as my Counselor and obeyed His guidance without finding that He followed it up as the Mighty One with His omnipotent working. The reason we do not more frequently find His power is because we try to turn it into the channels of our own wisdom instead of getting His mind, working in His will, and even knowing that we must have His effectual working. How blessed that the wonderful Counselor is always a child, and that His guidance offered to each of us is as simple, as accessible as the hand of a little child.

So let us walk in the Spirit, trusting His guiding hand, and committing all our ways to His wisdom and love.

4. If we would walk in the Spirit we must obey Him when He does speak, and we must remember that the first part of obedience is to hearken. It is not enough to say we have done all we knew. We ought to know, and we may know, for He has said that we shall know His voice, and if we do not it must be that we are to blame, or else God is responsible for our mistake. But this cannot be.

If we will be still and suppress our own impulses and clamorous desires, and will meet Him with a heart surrendered to His will and guidance, we shall know His way. "The meek will He guide in judgment, and the meek will He teach His way." The soul that walks in the Spirit will therefore be a hearkening spirit, watching daily at His doors, and longing to know His very commandments; and when we understand His voice we will implicitly obey it. The minding of the Spirit is life and peace. The very condition of His continual presence is obedience. "The Holy Spirit whom God hath given to them that obey Him." The secret of every cloud that has fallen upon the soul will probably be found in some neglected voice of our Monitor. He is waiting and has been waiting for us at that point where we have refused to follow, and when we step in His will we shall find Him there.

5. Walking in the Spirit implies that we shall keep step with the Holy Ghost, and that our obedience shall be so prompt that we shall never find ourselves a step behind Him, and following Him at a distance, from which we may find it hard to recover.

On our great railroads there are certain trains which run upon the highest possible schedule of time. The itinerary is so arranged that there is no margin allowed on which to overtake lost time, so that, should the train be late, it is scarcely possible to overtake the interval lost. God has drawn the plan of our life on such a scale that there are no minutes left blank, and if we lose one, the next has no margin to afford for its recovery. All that we can crowd into the future will be needed for the future itself, and therefore if we lose a step there is danger that we shall continue to be a step behind, and it will require the same exertion to keep up even a step behind as it would to walk abreast of God every moment.

Yonder mill-race needs just as much water to run at low as at high tide. The very same quantity of water, if kept up to the level of the wheel, will run all the ponderous machinery as that which on a lower level only wastes itself in fretting wavelets among the rocks of the torrent bed. And so it is just as easy for our spiritual life to move at the maximum as at the minimum if we only start at the right level, and so guard the moments that we shall not lose our headway, or get behind God. The secret of this one blessing is instant obedience and walking by the moment with Him in the fullness of His blessed will. Let us not disappoint Him. Let us not come short of all the good pleasure of His goodness. His thought for us is always best; His commandments "for our good always;" His schedule of our life-journey planned by unerring wisdom and unutterable love.

He has given us a gentle, patient Guide, who is willing to go with us all the way, and come into the minutest steppings of our life. Let us take heed that we grieve Him not away nor miss aught of His gentle will. Let us be sensitive to His touch, responsive to His whisper, obedient to His commandments, and able ever to say "He hath not left me alone, for I did always those things which please Him."

II. Some of the Blessings of thus Walking in the Spirit.

1. It will secure us a complete and delightful deliverance from sin. The expulsive power of His presence will drive out the presence of evil. "If we walk in the Spirit we shall not fulfill the lusts of the flesh." Our life shall thus be transformed from a defensive warfare, in which we are always attacking evil, to a glorious consciousness of God only, which shall exclude the evil from our thought as well as from our life. We shall not have to constantly clear the sunken rocks from our channel, but on the high and full torrent of the Divine life we shall rise far above every obstruction and move, as in Ezekiel's vision, in a river of life which shall be above the ankles, and above the loins, a river to swim in, carrying us by its own substantial fullness.

2. Such a walk will give a delightful serenity, tranquility, and steadfastness to our whole life. We shall not be at the bidding of impulses or circumstances, but shall move on in the majestic order of the Divine will, carried above the vicissitudes of failure and outward change, and fulfilling, like the stars in their courses, the full circle of His will for our life.

3. Such a walk will enable us to meet the providences of God as they come to us in victory, and to maintain the perfect harmony between our inward life and the outward leadings of His own. We have some beautiful examples of the transcendent importance of this walking in the Spirit, in connection with the conjunctures of circumstances on which so much often hangs. There never was a moment in human history on which more depended than that when the infant Christ was first brought into the Temple. What an honor and privilege it was to be there and catch the first glimpse of His blessed face, and even hold in the embrace of human arms the Gift of ages! Yet that was the honor of two aged pilgrims who were walking in the Spirit. Simeon and Anna, led of the Holy Ghost, came in at that very moment into the Temple. Led of God unerringly, and walking step by step with Him, they were enabled to meet Him in this glorious opportunity, and be the first heralds of His coming. No wonder the aged Simeon, as he took him in his arms, could ask no more on earth: "Lord, now lettest Thou Thy servant depart in peace, for mine eyes have seen Thy salvation."

Only less important was the crisis in the apostolic church when the gospel was to be preached for the first time to a new circle of disciples. The man chosen to carry the glad tidings to the Samaritans and the Gentiles, and to be the pioneer of Christianity among all the myriad tribes of the heathen world in that great progression of which the churches of Christendom today form the outcome, was a humble disciple, whom God could trust to walk in the Spirit and obey the slightest intimation of His will. It was Philip, the humble deacon. Already he had been sent to Samaria to preach the gospel in that city, no doubt in obedience to a similar Divine message. But, in the very height of his successful work in that city, the command suddenly comes to him to leave his work and go down to the desert of the South.

To most persons it would have seemed a misleading, a mistake, a neglect of providential duty, a waste of precious time, and an arresting of the great work in Samaria. But Philip immediately obeyed, and at every step of his journey he waited for new directions, and in due time the path was made plain. The first fruits of the heathen world were waiting at that very moment for his direction; and there on the crossroads of life, at the fitting moment, the Spirit brought those two men together, and the words were spoken in that chariot by the way, which changed the destiny of a life, and the course of a Dispensation, which opened the gospel to the whole world, and sent that Ethiopian prince to his home, to be, in all probability, the founder of many of those mighty churches, which for the next four centuries made Northern Africa the most important seat of ancient Christianity.

Yet, when his work with the eunuch was accomplished, the command was as distinct, to leave his new convert in the hands of the Lord, and follow on at the unknown leading of the same blessed Spirit that had brought them together." "The Spirit caught away Philip," we are told, "and the eunuch saw him no more." These are but some instances of the blessedness of this heavenly walk. Shall we trust our unseen Guide, and as we step out into the mysterious and momentous future, shall we walk more humbly, simply, instantly, and obediently in the companionship of His guiding hand?

Chapter 3: PERSON AND ATTRIBUTES OF THE HOLY GHOST

"God hath not given us the Spirit of fear, but of power, and of love, and of a sound mind." 2 Tim. 1: 7.

I. The Holy Spirit is a Person.

The Holy Ghost is a distinct individual, and not a vague influence, or a phase of Divine working.

Just as there are three judges on the bench, constituting the one court, three persons in the household, constituting the one family, so there are three distinct persons in the Godhead, yet forming together the one Deity, and more perfectly one in nature, volition, and action than it is possible for any created beings to harmonize.

The Holy Spirit is constantly spoken of in the Scriptures as possessing the attributes of a person. The personal pronoun is used to describe Him not it, but He; and the strongest and most distinctive of the Greek pronouns, that word 'autos,' which means 'himself,' and distinguishes personality, as no English term can, is often used of Him; as, for example, in 1 Cor. 12: 11, "That one and the self-same Spirit." Again, the attribute of will is ascribed to Him in the same passage, "as He will," and there is no stronger proof of personality than the power of choice. It is the most distinctive thing in any human being, and it is constantly attributed to the Holy Ghost.

Again, all the emotions proper to a person are ascribed to Him; He knows, loves, is grieved, is provoked, vexed, resisted, and, in short, is susceptible to all the feelings that are proper only for an intelligent person.

II. The Holy Spirit is a Divine Person.

This glorious Being is no less than God. He receives the divine names. Peter tells Ananias that in lying unto the Holy Ghost he has not lied unto men but unto God. Christ declares that in casting out devils by the Holy Ghost, He does it by the finger of God. He possesses Divine attributes; He is omniscient; "The Spirit searcheth all things;" omnipresent; "Whither shall I go from Thy Spirit, or hide from Thy Presence;" omnipotent; for Christ declares that, "The things that are impossible with men," namely, the salvation of the human soul, "are possible with God," and it is the Holy Ghost that converts the soul, therefore, He must have the omnipotence of God.

He is called the Holy Spirit, and holiness is a Divine attribute. Again, He performs the works of God; He was a partaker in the work of creation; the Spirit of light, order, beauty and life. He accomplishes the regeneration and sanctification of the soul which are divine works; He effected the incarnation and resurrection of the Son of God, and He will participate in the final resurrection of the saints of God from the tomb, at the Lord's coming.

Such works could be performed by no man, and they stamp Him as Divine. And, finally, He receives Divine worship; His name is associated with the Father and the Son in apostolic benediction, the formula of baptism, and the worship of the heavenly host. And John opens the Apocalypse with an ascription of praise, which links Him with the Father, and would be blasphemy if it were not Divine.

III. The Personal Attributes of the Holy Ghost.

Three of these only we shall mention. The three named in our text. "He is the Spirit of power, and of love, and of a sound mind."

1. His power. He is Almighty. Within the sphere of His special office and operations there is nothing He cannot do; there is no case too hard for His working, no soul too lost for Him to save, too hard for Him to soften, too vile for Him to sanctify, too weak for His use. He is the Spirit of creation. Look abroad upon the springing forces of nature, throbbing in the springtide of life and glory; how quietly, majestically and resistlessly nature is moving on to the resurrection of the year, to the fullness and glory of the summer and the harvest; how abundant and redundant the exuberant life and power we behold on every hand, covering the forest and the field with a wealth of luxuriance of flowers, and foliage, and fruitfulness, beyond the actual needs of earth's inhabitants; scattering with tropical bounty the gifts of God, as though His strength and love were so full He knew not how to find vent for all its overflow.

Why should He be less full, less bountiful, less Almighty in the realm of grace? Nay, larger and nobler still is His promise here. "I will pour water upon him that is thirsty, and floods upon the dry ground," is His blessed promise.

There is no stint to His resources. Let us enter into His omnipotence, and go forth knowing the might of our God, and claiming the full plentitude of His power and grace.

But mightier still is the power displayed in the resurrection of Jesus Christ. When the apostle would lift our conception up to an adequate realization of the hope of our calling and the riches of the glory of our inheritance, and the exceeding greatness of God's power to usward who believe, he points us to that transcendent miracle, the resurrection of Jesus Christ. He sees Him, without an effort, bursting the bonds of death, snapping asunder the sealed tomb, rising up above all the power of death and the natural law of mortality, above the laws of the material world, and passing through the closed door, and rising above the solid earth, as He triumphantly ascends above all might and dominion, far above all principality and power, higher and higher, till He is above the earth, above the sky, above the heavens, above every name that is named, not only in this world, but that which is to come. And then He sees us seated by His side, and raised up by the same Holy Spirit to share in all the fullness of Christ's ascension, glory and power. This is the measure of the power of grace; let us claim it in all its majestic fullness, and bring it down to lift up our life and the souls around us, to the heights of grace and glory.

2. Let us think of His love; it is greater than His power; all the terms in which He is described are notes of tenderness and expressions of gentleness, loveliness and grace. "I beseech you," says the apostle, "by the love of the Spirit." What love it was for Jesus Christ to live for thirty years and more in this uncongenial world, but oh! not less the love of the blessed Holy Ghost; He has lived for eighteen hundred years in this scene of sin, and this land of enemies.

How gentle the love of Jesus in coming so near to sinful men, but the Holy Ghost has come still nearer, but He enters our very hearts, and dwells in the inmost bosom of lost and worthless men. How marvelous the grace of Christ that endured the shame and spitting, the rejection and crucifixion of the Judgment Hall and the cross, but not less the gentleness which has pleaded for ages with wicked men, and borne all their resistance, rebellion and rejection, and yet waited through a whole lifetime to win the faintest response from their faith or love.

How much He has borne from each of us; how gently and patiently He has suffered our slights, endured our ignorance, stupidity, gross, and direct disobedience!

How close He is willing to come to the heart; how unreserved and condescending His intimacy and affection; how dear we are to His affection! None but His loved ones know how exquisite and intimate the communion which we may enjoy under His feathers and wings, and on the bosom of His love; telling Him all our sorrow and care, finding Him responsive to every whisper and breathing of our heart, and ever near, by day or by night, our blessed Paraclete, and ever present One, ready to help in every time of need.

He asks more of our trust and love: Oh! let Him not ask in vain. Let us know, and prove, and fully appreciate the love of the Spirit.

3. He is the Spirit of wisdom.

Not only can He give us wisdom, but with a wisdom greater than all that we may see, He is guiding, teaching, overruling all our life. Let us trust His wisdom, love, and power, and as we read these succeeding pages, yield ourselves with a glad " yes" to His every call, and know the full blessing of "Walking in the Spirit."

Chapter 4: OFFICES AND RELATIONS OF THE HOLY GHOST

I. The Holy Spirit in Relation to the Godhead.

This Divine person has a special place in the Trinity, and in the Divine economy.

With respect to the Father, He is spoken of as proceeding from Him; the same term is also used of His relation to the Son; He has been called the executive of the Godhead.

Many figures have been used; although all such figures must ever be unsatisfactory to illustrate the relation of the Divine persons. Perhaps the most successful is that which compares them to the various forms of light; primeval light, representing the Father; solar light, that is, light centered in an actual sun, representing the Son, and atmospheric light, that is, the light reflected and refracted, and turned into vision and illumination in the atmosphere and the world around us, the Holy Ghost, who brings to us the Divine Presence, and practically applies to us the benefits of God's revelation and grace.

His relation to the second person of the Godhead is very clearly revealed; it was He who ministered in His incarnation, and through whom He became the Son of Man as well as the Son of God. It was He who personally united Himself with the person of Christ, and became the power of all His miracles and teachings. It was He through whom "He offered Himself without spot to God." It was He through whom He arose from the dead. And after His resurrection it was by the Holy Ghost that He gave commandment to His apostles of all things concerning the kingdom of heaven. Again, it was in His own person that He received and shed forth the same Spirit of Pentecost upon His disciples, so that Jesus is ever identified with the Holy Ghost in all His work and ministry.

Nor is there any reason to suppose that He will be sent from the world in the millennial kingdom, but will be an actual and joyful witness of the blessed fruits of His own gracious working, as well as the Savior's suffering and death.

II. The revelation of the Holy Spirit to the world and the sinner.

"Whom the world cannot receive" is Christ's own explanation of his relation to the unsaved, "because it seeth Him not, neither knoweth Him." The Holy Ghost cannot dwell in an unconverted soul. On man's flesh the anointing oil could not be poured of old, nor can it still.

At the same time, He can and does work in the hearts of the unconverted, producing conviction and conversion, and leading them to a saving union with the person of Christ. This is His own special work; the sinful soul is dead in trespasses and sins, and it is His to quicken it, to convict of sin; and then of righteousness and judgment, and bring to the heart the revelation of Jesus, and, as it accepts Him, the assurance of pardon, the peace of God, and all the quickened graces of the new life in Christ.

III. This relation to the believer.

Having led the soul to Christ, the Holy Spirit now becomes the personal Guide, Teacher, Sanctifier and Comforter of the believer. His various ministries will be unfolded in the following chapters.

When the heart is fully surrendered to Him, He becomes its personal, permanent, indwelling Guest; bringing with Him the manifested presence of the Father and the Son, leading into all truth, guiding in all the will of God, supplying all the needed grace, unfolding the life of Jesus Christ in the believer's daily life, and developing all the fruits of the Spirit in their full variety and complete maturity.

He is the Spirit of light and revelation, of guidance, and of wisdom. He is the Spirit of holiness. He is the Spirit of peace, joy and comfort. He is the Spirit of love, gentleness, patience, meekness, and forbearance. He is the Spirit of prayer and intercession. He is the Spirit of power for service, and the source of all our gifts as well as graces. He is the Spirit of physical life and healing. He is the Spirit of faith and hope, enabling us to claim the promises of God, and revealing to us the glorious prospects of the future. Our whole spiritual life is nourished and cherished by His love and care; and all we are, and have, and may become, in our Christian life, is due to His personal indwelling, and His faithful love and infinite grace.

But in all His work in the believer's heart and life, He ever represents and reveals, not His own person or ours, but the Lord Jesus: He is the Spirit of Christ; "He shall testify of me; He shall glorify me," was the Master's own language; "for He shall take of the things that are mine, and shall show them unto you."

He reveals to us our personal union with Jesus and makes Christ actual to our consciousness. "At that day," that is when He comes, "ye shall know that I am in my Father, and ye in me, and I in you."

Like the telescope, which shows the observer, not its own beauty, but the heavenly orbs on which we gaze through its crystal lens, so the Holy Ghost becomes the invisible medium through whom we behold the face of Jesus, and are brought into the consciousness of His grace and fellowship.

Therefore, the soul is conscious of Christ, rather than the Spirit, even in the moment of His most blessed visitations. And yet we may be directly conscious of the Spirit also, and hold immediate fellowship with Him personally, receive the assurance of His love, and pour out into His heart our gratitude and affection.

IV. Relation to the Church.

Not only to the individual believer, but to the collective body of the people of God does the Holy Spirit specially come. It is He who constitutes the Church, and clothes her with the life and power of her Living Head. Until the day of Pentecost and the descent of the Spirit, the apostles were not permitted to go forth, and to speak and work for the Master.

The Holy Ghost is the very life and power of Christianity, and without Him the Church is like a ship without fire in her engine, or steam in her boiler; like an army of soldiers lying lifeless; like Ezekiel's vision in the plain; like a body without an animated soul.

The Church was never intended to be a natural and intellectual organization, but a supernatural instrumentality wholly dependent upon the direct power of God for all her efficiency, and therefore, needing to be ever separated from the arm of flesh and the strength of mere human agencies.

The Church in which the Holy Ghost abides is no mere sectarian fragment, but the whole body of believers united to Christ, the Living Head. "There is one body, even as ye are called in one hope of your calling, for by one Spirit are we all baptized into one body;" and though there be diversities of gifts, it is the same Spirit; differences of administrations, it is the same Lord; varieties of operations, it is the same God which worketh all in all. For to one is given, by the same Spirit, the word of wisdom; to another the word of knowledge, by the same Spirit; to another faith, by the same Spirit; to another the gift of healing, by the same Spirit; to another the working of miracles, to another prophecy, to another discerning of spirits, to another diverse kinds of tongues, to another the interpretation of tongues; but all these worketh that one and the self-same Spirit, dividing to every man severally as He will

For as the body is one and has many members, and all the members of that one body, being many, are one body; so also is Christ. For by one Spirit are we all baptized into one body, whether we be Jews or Gentiles, whether we be bond or free; and have been all made to drink into one Spirit. For the body is not one member, but many."

V. The Revelation of the Holy Spirit to the various Dispensations.

In all the dispensational periods of the past, the Holy Ghost has been present. Even in the antediluvian days, He strove with men. Under the Levitical economy He was present, qualifying the builders of the tabernacle for their work, anointing Moses, Aaron, and Joshua for their ministry, inspiring the ancient prophets for their messages, and enabling the individual believers of the Old Testament to know, believe, and obey God in the measure of their spiritual life.

But until after Christ's ascension the Holy Spirit was not personally resident as He is now. His influences were exercised upon the hearts of men, but His presence was not localized, as it has been since the day of Pentecost, in the body of Christ, the Church. Just as Queen Victoria exercises her influence over her Canadian provinces, but does not reside there, so the Holy Spirit was present in the world potentially, but not personally, as now.

Since the beginning of the Christian dispensation, however, he has resided on earth, and not in heaven, and is here locally, as the Lord Jesus was during His earthly life. The transcendent preeminence which a New Testament saint enjoys is, that his soul and body become the living and actual temple of the Holy Ghost.

This is the time of His special working; in an age when we may look for His unlimited operations, and toward the close of which we should anticipate the mightiest triumphs of His grace and power, as He shall usher in the next, namely, the millennial age, with the personal presence of Christ once more on earth, as in the days of His flesh.

But, even then, the Holy Ghost will not be absent. He will ever reside in the believer and the Church.

The question has been argued whether the Holy Spirit will be present on earth during the tribulation days, after the saints have been translated to be with the Lord in the air. We cannot doubt that He will still remain on earth, for how else could the Jewish remnant, who shall follow the Lamb, be converted, sustained and saved; also the Gentile remnant, who during those awful days shall turn to the Lord, including perhaps many of the members of a cold church who were not ready for the Master's coming at the time of His appearing?

We, therefore, cannot agree with the view of some; that when the saints are caught up to meet the Lord, the Holy Spirit shall be taken away from earth. We believe He has chosen this dark abode of sin and sorrow as the scene of His ceaseless, and ultimately triumphant labors, and that He shall yet rejoice over it as a restored and renovated realm, shining in all the loveliness, sinlessness and blessedness of His accomplished restoration.

Chapter 5: EMBLEMS AND ASPECTS OF THE HOLY SPIRIT

"The Seven Spirits which are before His Throne." Rev. 1: 4.

This expression denotes the fullness of the Holy Spirit. The number seven is expressive of divine completeness, and the benediction of the seven spirits is equivalent to the ascription of Paul in the first chapter of Ephesians: "Blessed be the God and Father of our Lord Jesus Christ, who hath blessed us with all spiritual blessings in heavenly places in Christ Jesus."

In keeping with this seven-fold expression of the Spirit's fullness, is the fact that we have seven special emblems of the Holy Spirit given us in the Scriptures, each fitted to emphasize some special phase of His character and work. As the Holy Ghost has no personal and incarnate form like Christ, He has clothed Himself in the robes of symbol, and thus becomes to us more real and vivid in the figures of human speech and earthly imagery.

I. The Dove

1. The earliest symbol of the Holy Spirit is the dove. Not in express terms is this figure introduced in the Old Testament, but the allusion in the opening verses of Genesis is sufficiently clear to be recognized. "The Spirit of God moved upon the deep;" literally this is translated, "The Spirit of God fluttered or brooded upon the face of the deep." It is the picture of the mother-bird spreading her wing over the stormy elements, and incubating, as it were, her brood through the dark night of chaos.

It is the same typical figure that we meet again as the emblem of peace and gentleness, and the herald of the morning of the new world in the dark and stormy night of the deluge. It is the same blessed person, who, on the banks of the Jordan, descended in visible form like a dove, and abode upon the Lord Jesus, the herald of peace and love to a sinful world, and the emblem of the Spirit of Christ's ministry. As the dove, the Holy Ghost is the Spirit of peace, the Giver of rest.

This is also a figure of motherhood, which is constantly associated with the picture of the blessed

Paraclete. In the Divine Trinity there is found the substance of all relationships, and that which is expressed in human motherhood must always have been in the bosom of God.

Of this the Holy Ghost is the personal expression. From that material breast our new life is born; by that gentle Spirit our spiritual childhood is nurtured, comforted, educated, developed, and matured. "As one who his mother comforteth," so doth the Comforter love and cheer our sorrowing hearts. As the brooding dove, so does this blessed One hide us beneath the wings of God, and cover us with the feathers of the divine sympathy and tenderness.

It is almost difficult to use the masculine form in speaking of this blessed person, so womanlike is the sweetness and softness of His touch.

His is that gentle voice we hear,

Soft as the breath of even,

That stills each doubt, and calms each tear,

And speaks to us of heaven.

II. Air is the next symbol of the Spirit.

This also appears in the opening chapter of Genesis. "The Lord God breathed into his nostrils the breath of life, and man became a living soul." And this we know was the Holy Spirit, for, we are told, "The inspiration of the Almighty giveth life." "Thou sendest forth thy Spirit, they are created."

The same figure is used by the prophet Ezekiel in describing the resurrection of the dry bones. It was the Spirit that came from the four winds and breathed upon the slain, and they lived. Our Lord has used this figure in two very striking connections. The first is in relation to the regeneration of a soul. "The wind bloweth where it listeth, and thou hearest the sound thereof, but canst not tell whither it cometh nor whither it goeth, so is every one that is born of the Spirit."

It is like the voiceless wind, known not by visible perception, but by its effects.

Again he uses it in connection with the personal imparting of the Holy Ghost to His own disciples. "He breathed on them and said, receive ye the Holy Ghost."

In keeping with this figure the Hebrew and Greek word is the same as that used for the wind, or the breath. The Holy Ghost is the breath of God. This emblem expresses at once the gentleness and the strength of the Holy Ghost. His coming may be as quiet as the evening zephyr, or mighty as the tempest's power. When He descended on Pentecost, there was a sound as of a mighty rushing wind; when He came afterwards to the assembled disciples, the place was shaken where they were assembled; when He answered the prayer of Paul and Silas the prison rocked to its foundation, and the bolts and bars were loosed.

But above all the manifestations of His tremendous power the most blessed is His quickening breath. This figure especially expresses the idea of life, the Spirit that breathes the new life in conversion, that imparts the very life of Christ to the soul, and quickens the mortal body into His resurrection power.

III. The water.

This emblem runs through the whole typology of the Old Testament, and the figurative language of the New.

This was the significance of the stream that flowed from Horeb's riven rock, and the diverse washings of the Levitical system. It was of this that Jesus spoke when He said, "He that believeth on me, out of him shall flow rivers of living water." It was of this that the prophet said, "I will pour water upon the thirsty, and floods upon the dry ground, and they shall spring up as among the grass, as willows by the water courses." This is the rain that comes upon the new-mown grass, and the dew which revives the earth. It is the fulness of the Holy Spirit in His cleansing, refreshing, and comforting influences. This is He who comes to us in the washing of regeneration, and the renewing of the Holy Ghost which He sheds upon us abundantly. This is He who sends the times of refreshing from the presence of the Lord. This is He who baptizes us in the ocean of divine light and love, and fills us with all the fullness of God.

IV. The Oil.

The oil is another Old Testament figure of the Holy Ghost, appearing in all the anointings of the priesthood and tabernacle, and reappearing in the very name of Christ, which means the anointed One. It was of this that He said, "the Spirit of the Lord is upon me; for He hath anointed me to preach the gospel. to the poor; He hath sent me to bind up the broken-hearted, to preach deliverance to the captives, the opening of the eyes to them that are blind, to preach the acceptable year of the Lord."

This figure describes the Holy Ghost as the figure of light, consecration, and healing.

In the ancient ritual, the head, hands, and feet of the cleansed leper and the consecrated priest were touched with oil as a symbol of their dedication to God. Thus Aaron was set apart, thus David was consecrated, and thus we are dedicated to Christ, and divinely qualified for service by the anointing of the Holy Ghost.

But the oil was also the figure of light in the vision of Zechariah. The temple is lighted by seven lamps that are fed by two living olive trees, teaching us that the Holy Ghost is the constant and living source of His people's life and light.

It is in this connection that John says, "But ye have an unction from the Holy One, and ye know all things. The anointing which ye have received of Him abideth in you, and ye need not that any man teach you; but as the same anointing teacheth you of all things, and is truth, and is no lie, and even as it hath taught you, ye shall abide in Him."

And so, also, the oil speaks of His healing touch. Oil and wine are used in the parable of the good Samaritan as figures of physical restoration.

And so the disciples anointed the sick and commissioned the elders to continue the same rite in the command, James 5: 14, as a token of the touch of the Holy Ghost upon the suffering form, and communicating to each the love of the Lord Jesus Christ.

Oil might also be used as a symbol of gladness. The Psalmist speaks of oil which makes our face to shine, and describes Jesus Christ as anointed with the oil of gladness above His fellows. Isaiah speaks of the oil of joy for mourning, and the garment of praise for the spirit of heaviness. The Holy Ghost anoints us with the spirit of joy, and He radiates the face with the reflected glory of the indwelling God.

Have we received the divine anointing as our light and healing, our joy and consecration? The oil that fell on Aaron's head descended to the skirts of his garments; and from our Great High Priest the divine anointing descends to His lowliest member.

Let us consecrate our hands and feet, our head and heart to be touched and dedicated from this holy chrism, and go forth as the Lord's anointed.

V. The Fire.

The mightiest of human forces is the last figure implied to represent the Holy Spirit up to the time of His descent at Pentecost. It had appeared in the very beginning in the Shekinah which hovered at Eden's gate; the pillar of fire that led the camp of Israel, the descending flame that consumed the sacrifices in the tabernacle, the blaze of the burning bush in Horeb, the coals of fire in Isaiah's vision, the glowing symbols of Ezekiel's imagery, the figurative language of John the Baptist prophesying of Him who should baptize with the Holy Ghost and with fire; and at length it was revealed in all its manifested meaning in the cloven tongues of Pentecost, and the fiery baptism of the assembled disciples.

It is the figure of destruction, reminding us of the Spirit which consumes not only the sin, but also the life of nature, and leaves the soul an empty vessel for the divine filling. It represents also, more emphatically than any other figure, the idea of cleansing; penetrating every fiber of our being, purifying with intrinsic power the inmost soul, and eliminating every particle of dross and evil.

This is also the figure of power, reminding us of the mightiest forces of human mechanics, electricity and steam, which are forms of fire, and the great dynamic center of our system, and the fiery sun which holds up the planets in their orbits by his power; so the Holy Ghost is the source of omnipotent power; impelling all the machinery of Christianity, moving all the forces of the soul, and enduing us with all we can ever know of power for service.

The fire is also the image of love; it is the force that melts, dissolves barriers, fuses hard substances, and welds the pieces into one.

And so the Holy Ghost is the Spirit of love, melting the stony heart, dissolving the prejudices of men, and uniting the people of God as one heart. It is His to give the glow of enthusiasm and the fire of holy zeal; it was He who clothed Elijah with his fervor, John with his love, Paul with his tremendous energy, Whitfield with his love of souls, and Fenelon, Rutherford and McCheyne with their seraphic piety.

Have we received the baptism of fire? It is the still unexhausted promise of the New Testament, waiting its mightiest manifestations just before the coming of the great and terrible day of the Lord.

VI. The Seal.

Another symbol has been added in the epistles, following with peculiar propriety the complexion of redemption, and the ratifying of the covenant by the death and resurrection of Jesus Christ, and the descent of the Holy Ghost.

It is the figure of the seal in the epistles of Paul. This figure is used respecting the work of the Holy Spirit upon the heart of the believer, "In whom after ye believed, ye were sealed with that Holy Spirit of promise."

And so again He says, "Grieve not the Holy Spirit by whom ye were sealed unto the day of redemption." The covenant completed, the will made effectual; it is fitting that the seal should be added. And this the Holy Spirit becomes, putting upon the heart the distinct stamp of Christ, touching and making divine things real and tangible as the impression upon the seal and the wax. This figure represents the idea of certainty and reality in connection with the work of the Spirit. There is such an experience in the Holy Ghost. It is not enough that we merely believe the truth, we may also know it and experience it. "We have known and believed," John says, "the love that God hath to us," and so the Holy Ghost becomes to us the witness to our consciousness of the reality of Divine things; enabling us to say, "I know Him whom I have believed;" "We know that He abideth in us by the Spirit that He hath given to us;" "We know that we have eternal life;" "We know that we have the petitions that we desired of Him."

It is very important that we do not reverse the order of this experience; it does not come before faith, but after it. "After ye believed, ye were sealed with the Holy Spirit of promise." We should not rest short of this blessed reality, and if we yield ourselves unto God in the surrender of consecration, and the simplicity of trust, we shall receive the touch of His blessed hand, and the stamp of His own personal presence, and the very image of His blessed face impressed upon our hearts, and be able to say, "He who hath sealed us and anointed us is God, who hath also established us, and given us the earnest of the Spirit in our hearts.

This leads us to the last symbol of the Spirit, namely:

VII. The Earnest.

This also is added in the epistles along with the seal, and after the descent of the Holy Ghost at Pentecost. These two last symbols seem especially appropriate as added ones, in view of their special significance with respect to the finished redemption of Christ, and His approaching advent. All the other aspects of the Spirit's work have been expressed by former emblems, but there is still one more, namely, the prophetic. "He shall show you things to come;" so Christ promised regarding the Comforter. He was to be the foretaste of all the yet unrevealed and unrealized hopes of the glorious future, and one more term was needed to express this; this is afforded in the word 'earnest.'

An earnest in ancient legal customs was a handful of soil bestowed upon the purchaser of a piece of real estate, containing a portion of the very ground that he had bought, as a solemn pledge of the whole estate which was to be delivered in due time. It was not a handful of soil from any estate, but it was from the very ground that he had bought, and it guaranteed the identity, certainty, and completeness of the transfer in due time.

In this sense the Holy Spirit is to show a sample and pledge of our future inheritance. All that we are to be and to enjoy He brings us now in foretaste and in limited measure, as a pledge that it shall be all delivered in the fullness of time, in all its completeness.

The term is used in a two-fold connection in the epistles; first, of our spiritual inheritance, which the Holy Ghost foreshadows in our hearts by the experience of His sanctifying, comforting, and quickening life; giving us the measure in which we are able to receive amid the limitations of our mortal life, a real foretaste of the felicities and glories of heaven.

But there is a second sense in which He is also an earnest, namely: in our mortal bodies, into which he brings the physical life of Christ as an earnest and foretaste of the physical resurrection. Thus we have the firstfruits of the Spirit as the pledge that we shall yet have the full redemption of the body. "He that hath wrought us for this self-same thing," that is, for the future resurrection, "is God, who hath also given us the earnest of the Spirit."

Have we received this blessed token, and do we have in our measure all its meaning, in anticipation of the things which "eye hath not seen, ear hath not heard, and it hath not entered into the heart of man what God hath prepared for them that love Him," but of which it is added, "God hath revealed them unto us by His Spirit, for the Spirit searcheth all things, yea, the deep things of God?"

Can we claim the benediction of the seven Spirits which are before the throne, and say with the apostle, "Blessed be God, even the Father of our Lord Jesus Christ, who hath blessed us with all the blessings of the Spirit in heavenly places in Christ Jesus?"

Chapter 6: THE SPIRIT OF LIGHT

"Now we have received not the spirit of the world, but the Spirit which is of God; that we may know the things that are freely given to us of God." 1Cor. 2: 12.

The first aspect in which the Holy Spirit is revealed to us is as the Illuminator and Guide of our life. Even in the story of creation the first result of His brooding over the face of the deep is the command, "Let there be light." He is the Creator of the human mind and the Source of all the true light of reason and natural religion in the world; and He is the true Source of spiritual light. One of His special emblems is the oil and the seven-fold lamp of the temple.

I. He Gives the Light of Truth.

He has inspired the Holy Scriptures, the revelation of God's will, and the invaluable light that shines upon the heart of man, the pathway of the unseen world. The Bible is a standard of spiritual truth, and in all His teachings and leadings, the Holy Ghost never contradicts His own word. They who are more fully led of the Spirit will always most reverence the authority of the

Scriptures, and walk in the most perfect conformity with their principles and precepts.

But it is not enough to have the letter of the word, He who gave it must also interpret it and make it Spirit and life. It is His to unfold to the heart the power and reality of the written word and to bring it to our remembrance in the opportune moment as the lamp of guidance, or the sword of defense in the hour of temptation. "He will bring all things to your remembrance whatsoever I have said unto you." This is the blessed ministry of the personal Holy Spirit, and they who thus walk with Him shall find the Bible an ever new volume and the very light of life.

A prominent member of the House of Representatives, speaking the other day about the inestimable value of the National Library of Congress, was asked how it was possible for a busy member, without much study and labor, to know how to use it effectually, and to be able always to find the right volume or page where a given subject was discussed: "O," he replied, "that is made perfectly easy for us by our invaluable librarian who knows every book and subject, and all we have to do is to send a little page from our desk in the House with a note to him requesting the best authority on any subject we require, and he immediately comes back with the right book and the leaves turned down at the very spot where we need the information." Blessed be God, we have a Divine Librarian who understands the Bible better than we ever can, and who has come to be our Monitor and Guide, not only into its meaning, but also into its practical application to every need of life. "And if we walk in the Spirit He will guide us into all truth, and bring all things to our remembrance whatsoever Christ hath said unto us."

II. The Light of Revelation.

It is not enough to have a good light, we must also have the organs of vision or it is of no use; and we must have them in perfect condition. Now, the Holy Spirit comes to be to us sight as well as light; and as we walk in Him we shall be enabled to know the will of God as revealed in the Scriptures by a true spiritual apprehension, and from the very standpoint of God's own mind and thought.

In the chapter from which our text is taken the apostle uses a very fine analogy:

"No man," he says, "knoweth the things of a man except a spirit of a man which is in him; even so, knoweth no man the things of God except the Spirit of God is in us." You might sit down and talk to your little dog about the latest book, and explain to him in the clearest manner its wonderful teachings, and he would not understand a word; not from any defect in the truth, but because he had not the mind of a man to understand the things of a man; and so you might sit down and talk to the natural intellect about spiritual truth, even the brightest human intellect, and they would not comprehend it because it belonged to a higher sphere.

The only way by which that dog could understand you would be for you to impart to him a human mind, and the only way that man can understand the things of God is for God to impart to him the divine mind; therefore, the apostle says, "The natural man receiveth not the things of the Spirit, for they are foolishness unto Him; neither can he know them for they are spiritually discerned; but we have the mind of Christ."

This is the special work of the Holy Ghost, to give to us a new spiritual vision and organ of apprehension; so that the soul directly perceives divine things and realities. Perhaps the first effect of this divine illumination is that the things of God become intensely real, and stand out with vividness and distinctness, like figures cut in relief on the wall. The person of Christ, the light of His countenance, the distinct sweetness of His Spirit, the "peace that passeth all understanding," the joy of the Lord, the heavenly world, all become to the heart more actual and intensely vivid than the things we see with our outward eyes, and touch with our human hands; so that we can say of Christ with the apostle, "That which we have seen with our eyes, which we have looked upon, and our hands have handled of the Word of Life." This is the true meaning of this whole chapter. It is not a description of heavenly glories which we are going to see by-and-by, but of present revelations which the natural eye hath not seen, the material ear hath not heard, and the human heart hath not conceived: but which "God hath revealed to us by His Spirit; for the Spirit searcheth all things, yea, the deep things of God."

In the first chapter of Ephesians, the apostle Paul has given us a sublime view of the effect of this inward illumination upon the heart. "I cease not," he says, "to make mention of you in my prayers, that the God of our Lord Jesus Christ, the Father of glory, may give unto you the Spirit of wisdom and revelation in the knowledge of Him." "The eyes of your heart being enlightened that ye may know what is the hope of His calling, and what the riches of the glory of His inheritance in the saints."

"And what is the exceeding greatness of His power to us-ward who believe, according to the working of His mighty power."

"Which He wrought in Christ, when He raised Him from the dead, and set Him at His own right hand in the heavenly places,"

"Far above all principality, and power, and might and dominion, and every name that is named, not only in this world, but also in that which is to come;"

"Which is His body, the fullness of Him that filleth all in all."

"And hath raised us up together, and made us sit together in heavenly places in Jesus Christ;"

"That in the ages to come He might show the exceeding riches of His grace, in His kindness toward us through Christ Jesus. "

Here we find it is not the eyes of our intellect, but the eyes of the heart that are to be illuminated, and when so quickened by the Spirit of revelation in the knowledge of Him, we shall understand what is the hope of our calling, and glorious privileges and prospects which we are to inherit in Christ.

The riches of the glory of His inheritance are not only for us, but even in us now. We shall be stirred with a realization of the exceeding greatness of His power toward us and for us. We shall rise to an adequate conception of the mighty things that we may dare to claim of Him; especially shall we see the full meaning of Christ's resurrection and ascension. We shall see Him lifted up, not only above the grave and the burden of our guilt and sin, but far above all beings, all forces of natural law, all might and dominion, and every name that is named, up to the very throne of God where all things are under His feet. Not only so, but we shall see ourselves lifted above our sins, and fears, and sorrows, and enemies, and difficulties, and imperfections, until we, too, are sitting with Him far above all principality, might and dominion, in the heavenly places in Christ Jesus, as safe and triumphant as if we were already in heaven and had been there for ten thousand years.

Oh! such a view takes the sting out of life and stimulates to higher aspirations and victories, conflicts and service. But we must first perceive our inheritance before we can claim it, and as we look out upon all the fullness of His promise and provision we arise and walk through the land in all the length and breadth of it and make it our own. Under this divine light the promise of God grows strangely real, and the heart swells with faith and confidence. Doctrines which in the abstract we could not understand become simple and living realities. The profound truth of the Trinity changes into the personal and sweet fellowship of the Father, the Son, and the Holy Ghost. The doctrine of sanctification ceases to perplex and discourage, and becomes a simple experience of union with Jesus and abiding in Him. The mightiest supernatural works of Christ even in our bodies cease to be strange and incredible. The doctrine of His personal coming becomes a bright and personal expectation, and the whole world of spiritual things is more real to us in our own consciousness.

Sometimes the vision opens upon our own hearts and we are permitted to see their failures, imperfections, and needs; but under the light of God this is never discouraging because there always comes with it the revelation of Him who is the supply of every need and the provision for every defect in sin. Satan's pictures of our sins are terrible and always depressing; but the light of heaven reveals our errors only to heal them, and brings such sweetness and rest that we can only thank Him for making greater room for His all-sufficiency.

Sometimes, too, the curtain is lifted upon the heavenly world, and some souls whom God can trust are permitted, like Paul, to be brought so near that they behold what it were unlawful for a man to utter, and know not whether they are in the body or out of the body. Let no one covet such experiences, for they bring with them many a thorn in the flesh, lest we be exalted above measure. And above all let us not seek, with morbid curiosity, to intrude into things which belong not to our simple sphere of humble duty, but rather seek the light that is practical and useful.

And yet, if God gives the higher visions at times, and even lifts the veil of things to come for humble and holy souls who dwell hard by the gates of heaven, let us not wonder or question; and let them use such glimpses of glory as the mariner uses the burst of sunlight that sometimes pierces through the skies that have been clouded for weeks, and sails, by the observations of that hour, through all the coming days of cloud and storm.

III. The Light of Guidance.

The Holy Spirit is promised to us as our personal Guide in the path of life. "As many as are led of the Spirit they are sons of God." Some persons are so zealous for the word of God that they deny any direct guidance of the Spirit apart from the Word, but if we truly believe the Word itself we will be forced to accept its distinct statements, that the personal presence of God is given to the humble and obedient disciple for the needed direction in every step of life. "I will instruct thee in the way that thou shalt go; I will guide thee with mine eye." The Lord shall guide thee continually: "When He putteth forth His own sheep He goeth before them and they know

His voice." "In all thy ways acknowledge Him and He shall direct thy paths."

We find the apostle Paul constantly recognizing the personal direction of the Holy Spirit even in matters where there was no distinct direction in the Word. The whole course of Paul's missionary journeys was ordered by the personal direction of the Lord. Being sent forth, we are told, by the Holy Ghost, he and Barnabas sailed unto Cyprus. A little later the same Spirit restrained them from preaching in Bithynia and Asia, and led them from Troas to Philippi to begin their European ministry. Still later, we are told that he purposed in the Spirit to go to Jerusalem and Rome, and none of the perils of the way could afterward turn him aside from that which had come to him as the voice of God. No life was ever more practical, sensible, and scriptural than Paul's, and yet none more constantly recognized the supernatural direction of the Holy Ghost. The methods of divine guidance are various.

1. The Spirit guides us by the Scriptures, by their general principles and teachings, and by bringing to us special passages from the Word, either through the law of mental suggestion, and impressing them upon our heart, or by various ways fitted to emphasize a passage as a divine message to our hearts.

2. He also directs us by His own direct voice when necessary; and yet we must not expect the special and remarkable intimations of the Holy Ghost at all times, or when we have sufficient light from other sources. There is danger of fanaticism here. We have no right to ask God to give us a special revelation of His will where either the light of our own common sense or the teaching of Scripture have already made the matter sufficiently plain. For example: It would be foolishness to expect the Lord to show us by a direct message whether we ought to get up in the morning, to take our proper food, to attend to our daily business, to keep the Sabbath, or to perform the ordinary acts of kindness, courtesy and necessity; to pay our debts, to love our neighbor. All these things the Spirit has already told us, and it would be an impertinence to expect Him to come with a new revelation every time.

So, also, we cannot expect the Holy Spirit to reveal to us directly whether God will forgive us our sins, or sanctify our souls, because these things He has already explicitly promised us, and we can expect no added witness of the Spirit until we have first believed and acted upon His Word; then the Spirit will follow this by a confirming voice and a sweet inward assurance of the fulfillment of His promise. Many persons expect the Spirit to come to them with the assurance of forgiveness and salvation before they have even believed the promises that He has already spoken.

So also, we may add in regard to prayer for physical healing. When we are living in accordance to His Word it does not require a special revelation of the will of God, but that we should believe the revelation already made in the Scriptures, in His promises of healing through faith in Christ. But, where the matter is one on which the Scriptures have not spoken distinctly, and the circumstances are so peculiar as to require direct and new light, He has distinctly promised that He will lead us in the right way wherein we shall not stumble. He has said, "If in anything we be otherwise minded, and our views and ideas be mistaken, He will reveal even this unto us."

3. The Holy Spirit guides us most frequently by intuitions of our sanctified judgment, and the conclusion of our minds, to which He leads us with the quiet assurance of acting in perfect

freedom and naturalness, and yet of being influenced by the presence and suggestion of His own Spirit. Under such circumstances the mind and judgment are perfectly simple and natural. The thoughts come as our own, with delightful tranquility, and a certainty, and a sort of intuition that it is the right thing to do, and yet the secret consciousness that it is not our wisdom, but has been somehow reflected upon the soul by another. It is not so much the Spirit speaking to us as the Spirit speaking with us as part of our very consciousness, so that it is not two minds, but one.

The truly consecrated spirit may expect to be thus held and influenced by the Divine wisdom; and it will often find itself restrained from things by an inward reluctance, or repulsion, which it cannot fully explain, and led to other things by a strong and distinct inclination and sense of rightness and fitness which afterwards prove, by the result, to have been the directing presence of God. Of course, as we shall see immediately, there must be real consecration and holy vigilance in such a walk, to guard against our own impressions and inclinations in cases where they are not the intimations of the Spirit's will.

4. We are sometimes taught that we are guided by providences. A devout mind will, of course, always have regard to the external providences of God, and will be habitually watching to see His hand in everything that occurs; but it would be very dangerous to allow ourselves to be directed by outward events apart from the distinct leadings of God in our spirit and by His Word. Quite as frequently we shall find ourselves led to go in the face of circumstances as to follow the favoring gales of outward events. Most of the important events and accomplished purposes in the lives of God's servants, as recorded in the Scriptures, were in direct opposition to all the circumstances that were occurring around them. Take, for example, the life of David. From the very first time that he received the call of God to recognize himself as Israel's future king, everything in his life for nearly ten years seemed to conspire to forbid any such expectation.

Take again the life of Paul. We find him directly led by the Holy Spirit to cross the Hellespont and begin his ministry in Greece. But instead of being met by open doors and favoring circumstances, everything opposed, until at last he found himself scourged and bound, a helpless prisoner in a Roman dungeon. Had he been watching for the guidance of circumstances he would have concluded that he had made a mistake, and would have hastened to get away; but on the contrary, the more firmly believed that God had led him, and ere long the very circumstances were conquered and transformed by the victorious power of faith. So again, he was led to Jerusalem and Rome, but from that moment everything opposed him. All along the way the people of God even seemed to throw themselves across his path.

At Ephesus, they wanted him to remain to preach the gospel in the very place where a year before he had in vain tried to enter; but instead of recognizing this as a providence that ought to change his purpose he quietly deferred his work in Ephesus and pressed on to Jerusalem. Again and again on his way did the very prophets of the Lord warn him against visiting Jerusalem, and plead with him to abandon the dangerous purpose which would perhaps cost him his life; but he only replied "What mean ye to weep and to break mine heart? I am ready not only to be bound, but also to die at Jerusalem for the name of the Lord Jesus." Arriving at Jerusalem all that had been intimated comes to pass. Instead of being received by his countrymen, he is mobbed and well nigh killed, but he still presses on and the Lord meets him at night in his dungeon to assure him of His protection and direction.

Next, he is detained at Caesarea for two whole years languishing in a prison; but, instead of doubting his divine direction he presses steadily on, and uses the delay as an occasion of service for the Master. At length he has embarked for Rome; but even then the storm pursues him and the wild Euroclydon threatens to engulf him in the depths of the sea; but he falters not in his purpose, but rises majestically above the storm and carries even the lives of his fellow passengers, on the wings of his mighty faith, above disaster and destruction. Narrowly saved from shipwreck on the shores of Malta, a viper from the ashes springs upon his hand, and it seems as though earth and hell had determined to prevent his reaching Rome, but he only flings it off and suffers no harm, and so at length he marches up the Appian way more like a conqueror than a prisoner, thanking God and taking courage, as he realizes that not one word of all God's promise and direction has failed. Thus must we ever interpret the providences of God; instead of yielding to opposition, or following that which seems to favor us, press firmly on in the path of conviction and obedience, and our way shall be established, and our very difficulties become the occasions of our greatest triumphs.

Let us notice also some of the principles and conditions of divine guidance.

The first is a surrendered spirit. Before we can know His will we must always first yield our own. "The meek will He guide in judgment, and the meek will He teach His way."

Next, there must be a readiness to obey. He will not give us light unless we mean to follow it; to do so would only add to our condemnation. "If any man will do His will he shall know." "Then shall we know if we follow to know the Lord."

Secondly, we must trust His guidance; we must believe that He is with us and directing us. We must lean upon His arm with all our heart, and implicitly look up into His face and expect Him to be true to us. We must also have "our senses exercised by reason of use, to know the difference between good and evil." Sometimes our mistakes will become most instructive to us by showing us the places where we have erred, and save us from repeating the mistake afterwards with more serious consequences. We must learn to distinguish between mere impressions and the deeper convictions of the entire judgment under the light of the Spirit, and between the voice of the Shepherd and that of the spirit of error. This He will teach us, and teach us more and more perfectly through experience. We shall have to learn also to walk with Him when we cannot understand the way. His path is often a way that we have not known, and the answer to our prayer may seem to lead us directly contrary to our expectation and to the ultimate issue.

Once in my life I was led to ask the Lord for a special building as a residence, and received full assurance that it would be given; almost immediately afterwards it was sold to a person who insisted on occupying it himself, and refused under any circumstances to part with it. After much prayer I was led to consent, most unwillingly, to accept, instead of the house I had most desired, another owned by this very man. So distasteful was it to me that on the night I went to sign the lease I walked repeatedly past the door before I could bring myself to enter. At length, in simple obedience to the Holy Spirit, I did, but, to my surprise, the man met me and said that very afternoon he had been led to change his mind. While attending the funeral of an old friend a strange dread came over him about occupying the house that he had purchased and he had just decided to let me have it on terms more favorable than I could have expected had not God interposed. Thus, as I went forward in the path of simple obedience, by a way that I could not understand the true way opened up, and it was only blessing and delight. The most remarkable feature of it was that the house thus given became afterwards the place where all the work of the Lord, in which we are now engaged, began. God thus signally chose the place for His work, and put His seal upon it as a pattern of the providences which we should afterwards expect. So, still, "through fears, through clouds, through storms, He gently clears our way."

Let us trust His guiding hand, and follow the Lamb whithersoever He goeth.

IV. Light for Service.

"It is not ye that speak but the Spirit of your Father that speaketh in you." "I will give you a mouth and wisdom which all your adversaries shall not be able to gainsay nor resist." "If any man speak, let him speak as the oracles of God. If any man minister, let him do it as of the ability which God giveth, that God may be glorified through Jesus Christ." "Say not I am a child, for thou shalt go to all that I shall send thee, and whatsoever I command thee thou shalt speak." "And the Lord put forth His hand and touched my mouth; and the Lord said unto me, behold! I have put my words in thy mouth." "The Lord God hath given me the tongue of one that hath been instructed that I might know how to speak the Word in season to him that is weary." "He openeth my ear morning by morning to hear as one that is instructed." This was the secret of even Christ's ministry. "The Word that I speak is not mine, but the Father's which sent me." "As I hear I speak."

Before we can speak God's messages we must learn to listen. The opened ear comes before the opened mouth. It is very hard sometimes to die to our own thoughts and elaborate preparations for service, and to be free and open for God to use us as vessels meet for the Master's use. Sometimes He has to humble us by showing us the barrenness of all our best intellectual work, and then lead us to receive the living messages of His Holy Spirit. Sometimes we may think the message very unworthy and almost unsuitable, but God loves to take "the things that are not to bring to nought the things that are, that no flesh may glory in His presence."

A saintly spirit whom God has greatly used in personal messages, tells how once she was distinctly sent by the Lord on a certain train; but when she arrived at the station the train was crowded and the guard told her she could not go. Still she waited, having learned that a point-blank refusal is often the best evidence of God's working; but just as the train was about to leave, suddenly the guard came to her and hurried her into a carriage which had just been put on. There she found herself sitting beside a young gentleman, and immediately the thought came, "This is the service the Lord has sent me to do." After a little she introduced the subject of personal religion, but he haughtily replied, "My family object to my being talked to on such subjects." "My dear sir," she replied, "I had supposed that this was not a question for your family, but for yourself." "Then," he answered, still more stiffly, "I object to be talked to on such questions." It seemed as though the way of service was blocked, and yet the unerring Spirit had led her there.

Then the thought came that she should give him a tract, and that God would bless the silent messenger even after they had parted. But as she searched through all her pockets she found she had forgotten all her tracts. Suddenly, amid her movements, her valise fell on the floor, and all its contents were poured in disorder at their feet. With the instincts of a gentleman he helped her to pick up the wreck, when suddenly her eye fell upon a single tract that had fallen out with the other articles; but as she picked it up she felt, why, this will never do, for it was a tract especially addressed to a young man that had just been saved from shipwreck. But the same unerring Guide whispered to her to put it in his hands and ask him to read it.

He took it, having grown a little freer, through their better acquaintance, and as he read the title his face became deadly pale. Before he had read the second page the tears were pouring down his cheeks. "Madam," he cried, turning to her, "who told you about me?" "Why, no one," she answered, "what do you mean?" "Why," said he, "Some one must have told you; did you not know that only last week I was rescued from shipwreck?" It was the arrow of the Infinite One whose wisdom never fails, and the humble worker, waiting His bidding, had not been suffered to err. The message reached his heart, and ere they parted he was saved. This is the true secret of effectual service, and when He becomes to us the Wonderful Counselor, we shall always find Him also the Mighty God.

Chapter 7: THE SPIRIT OF HOLINESS

"Elect according to the foreknowledge of God the Father, through sanctification of the Spirit, unto obedience and sprinkling of the blood of Jesus Christ." 1 Peter 1: 2.

It would throw a flood of light on the perplexing doctrine of election if we would remember, when thinking of this subject, that we are elected by God, not unto salvation unconditionally and absolutely, but unto holiness. We are predestined to be conformed to the image of His Son. It is idle and unscriptural, therefore, to talk about being elected to salvation irrespective of our faith or obedience. We are elected to obedience and sprinkling of the blood of Christ, and are summoned, therefore, to make our calling and election sure, by pressing on into the fullness of the grace of Christ. This work of sanctification is especially the work of the Holy Spirit. Let us look carefully at the principles that lie at the foundation of it, and its connection with the person and work of the Holy Ghost.

1. The holiness to which we are called, and into which we are introduced by the Holy Spirit, is not the restoration of Adamic perfection, or the recovery of the nature we lost by the fall. It is a higher holiness, even the very nature of God Himself, and the indwelling of Jesus Christ, the second Adam, to whose perfect likeness we shall be restored through the work of redemption. We are predestined to be conformed to the image of His Son. This will determine all our subsequent conclusions in the consideration of this subject. Sanctification is not the perfection of human character, but the impartation of the divine nature, and the union of the human soul with the person of Christ, the new Head of redeemed humanity.

2. Our sanctification has been purchased for us through the redemption of Christ. By one offering He has perfected forever all them that are sanctified. When He came He said, "Lo! I come to do thy will, O God; yea, thy law is in my heart, by which will we are sanctified through the offering of the body of Jesus Christ once for all."

Our sanctification, therefore, as well as our justification, was included in the finished work of Christ, and it is a free gift of His grace to every ransomed soul that accepts it, in accordance with His word and will. It is one of our redemption rights in Christ, and we may claim it by faith as freely as our forgiveness. "For He gave Himself for us that He might redeem us from all iniquity, and purify unto Himself a peculiar people, zealous of good works."

3. It is the office of the Holy Spirit to lead us into the full redemption of Jesus Christ, and therefore, into holiness. In pursuance of this heavenly calling, the Holy Spirit leads us first to see our need of sanctification. This He does by a two-fold revelation. First, He shows us the divine will for our sanctification, and the necessity for our becoming holy if we could please God. By nature and tradition many persons are prone to take a very different view of this subject, and to regard the experience of holiness as a sort of exceptional life for a few distinguished Christians, but not expected of all the disciples of Christ. But the awakened and startled mind discovers, in the light of Scripture and of the Holy Spirit, the falseness of this delusion, and the inflexible terms in which God's Word requires that all His people should be holy in heart and life. In the searching light of truth it trembles as it reads, "Without holiness no man shall see the Lord." "Into heaven there entereth nothing that defileth, nor worketh abomination, nor maketh a lie." "Blessed are they that wash their robes that they may have right to the Tree of Life and may enter in through the gates into the city." "He that walketh uprightly and worketh righteousness shall see the King in His beauty and behold the land that is very far off." "Who shall ascend unto the hill of the Lord or stand in His holy place? He that hath clean hands and a pure heart." "Be ye holy even as I am holy; be ye therefore perfect even as your Father in heaven is perfect." "These things have I written unto you that ye sin not. He that abideth in Him sinneth not; he that sinneth hath not seen Him neither known Him."

At this point the soul is compelled to face a very solemn crisis; either it must accept the Word of God literally and implicitly, or it must turn it aside by human tradition, and explain away its most plain and emphatic teachings, and render it of no effect in any of its promises or commands, and so enter upon a course which must end in practical infidelity. The latter alternative is taken by many; they content themselves with saying such a standard is impossible, nobody has ever reached it, and God does not actually mean it or require it. The result is that henceforth the Word of God becomes uncertain to them in all its messages, a practical faith ceases to be possible. But the other alternative drives the soul, if honestly faced, to self-despair; it can find no such holiness in itself, and no power to produce it.

The first effect, it is true, generally is to stir up the awakened heart to attempt a better life and try to work out a holiness such as God requires. Resolutions, outward amendments, perhaps many inward exercises, self-examinations, purposes of righteousness, and holiness, are the result. But in a little while there is a certain issue of failure and disappointment; perhaps the man becomes a Pharisee and deludes himself into the idea that he is complying with the divine standard. But, if the Holy Ghost is doing His office work thoroughly, he will soon become disgusted with his own righteousness, and find his utter inability even to reach his own standard. Some crucial test will come which he cannot meet, some command which strikes at the roots of his natural inclinations and requires the sacrifice of his dearest idols, and the poor heart will break down, and the will will shrink or rebel.

This was the experience of the apostle Paul; for the time he thought that he had attained unto the righteousness of the law, but when the commandment came, sin revived, and he died. The Lord said "Thou shalt not covet," and instantly his throbbing heart awoke with all the intensity of its natural life, to a thousand evil desires, all the stronger because they were forbidden, until in despair he cried out "I know that the law is spiritual, but I am carnal." "O wretched man that I am! who shall deliver me from the body of this death?" Ah! this is the very preparation for sanctification. He is just on the verge of deliverance. He has found at length his helplessness. He has got down to the bottom of the ladder of self-renunciation. It is to such a soul that the Master is saying, "Blessed are the poor in spirit, for theirs is the kingdom of heaven." "Blessed are they that hunger and thirst after righteousness, for they shall be filled."

So of old, God came to Job in the revelation of his own worthlessness until he cried, "I abhor myself." So He came to Isaiah, just before his cleansing, until the prophet smote upon his breast and cried, "Woe is me! for I am a man of unclean lips." Happy the heart that can see itself at its worst, without, on the one hand attempting to excuse its failure, or on the other, giving up in despair. For such a soul the Holy Spirit waits to bring the next stage of His blessed work of sanctification namely:

4. The revelation of Jesus Christ Himself as our sanctification. It is the purpose of God that the person of Jesus shall be to us the embodiment of all that there is in God and salvation. Therefore, sanctification is not a mere human experience or state, but is the reception of the person of Christ as the very substance of our spiritual life. For He "is made unto us of God, wisdom, righteousness, sanctification, redemption." It is not a wealthy friend advancing us the money to pay our debts, but it is the friend coming into our business and assuming it Himself, with all its burdens and liabilities, while we simply become subordinate and receive all our needs henceforth from Him. This was the glad cry which Paul sent back the moment he had reached the depths of self-despair: "I thank God through Jesus Christ our Lord." It is the Holy Spirit's function to reveal Him. "He shall take of the things of Christ and show them to us."

And so in the light of His revealing we behold Christ, the perfect One, who walked in sinless perfection through the world in His incarnation, waiting to come and enter our hearts, and dwell in us, and walk in us, as the very substance of our new life, while we simply abide in Him, and walk in His very steppings. It is not merely imitating an example, but it is living in the very life of another. It is to have the very person of Christ possessing our being; the thoughts of Christ, the desires of Christ, the will of Christ, the faith of Christ, the purity of Christ, the love of Christ, the unselfishness of Christ, the single aim of Christ, the obedience of Christ, the humility of Christ, the submission of Christ, the meekness of Christ, the patience of Christ, the gentleness of Christ, the zeal of Christ, the works of Christ, manifest in our mortal flesh, so that we shall say, "I live, yet not I, but Christ liveth in me." When the Holy Spirit thus reveals Him to the heart we can surely say, as a saint once said after such a vision, "I have had such a sight of Christ that I never can be discouraged again."

5. But the Spirit not only reveals Christ, but He actually brings him to occupy and abide in the heart. It is not enough to see, we must receive Him and become personally united to Him through the Holy Ghost. In order to do this there must be, on our part, a complete surrender and self-renunciation, followed by a definite act of appropriating faith. By it we receive the Lord Jesus Christ, and become filled with the Holy Ghost. In both of these we are led and enabled by the Holy Spirit. Through His gracious influence we present our bodies a living sacrifice, yield ourselves unto God in unreserved consecration, hand over to Him the old life of self and sin to be slain and buried forever, and offer ourselves to His absolute ownership, possession, and disposition, unconditionally and irrevocably. The more definite and thorough this act of surrender, then the more complete and permanent will be the result. It is true that, at the best, it

will be an imperfect consecration, and will need His merits to make it acceptable, but He will accept a sincere and single desire, and will add His own perfect consecration to our imperfect act, thus making it acceptable to the Father through His grace.

It is most blessed to know that in the very first act of a consecrated life we are not alone, but He Himself becomes our consecration, as He will afterwards become our obedience, and our strength step by step to the end. Having thus surrendered ourselves to Him for His sanctifying grace, we must next accept Him in His fullness that He does become to us henceforth all that we take Him for, and that we are now owned, accepted, possessed, cleansed and sanctified by His indwelling, and that He is saying to us, and, recording our glad amen, without reserve, to every word of it. "Now are ye clean through the word that I have spoken unto you." "The blood of Jesus Christ cleanseth us from all sin."

6. The Holy Spirit next seals this act of union by His own manifested presence, and He makes us know that we have the abiding of Jesus by the witness of His presence, and the baptism of His love and power. Before, however, we can expect to receive this, we must simply believe the promise of Christ, resting in the certainty of our acceptance and consecration, and begin to act by implicit faith in Him as already in our hearts. When we do so, the Holy Ghost will not withhold the conscious witness of our blessing a moment longer than is really necessary for the testing and establishing of our faith.

He will become to us a most blessed and personal reality, and it shall be true of us, as the Master Himself promised, after the Comforter has come, "at that day ye shall know that I am in the Father, and ye in me, and I in you." The soul will be filled with the delightful consciousness of the presence of God, sometimes as the Spirit of ineffable rest and holy serenity, sometimes as the Spirit of unutterable holiness, filling the heart as with the searching and consuming fire of divine purity. Sometimes the consciousness will be that of an intense hatred of sin, and a spirit of self-renunciation and holy vigilance. Sometimes it will be a spirit of love, an intense consciousness of the divine approval, and of God's delight in us and love to us, until the heart is melted with the sense of His tenderness. Sometimes it is a Spirit of unspeakable joy and rapture, continuing for days together, until the very tides of God's bosom seem to swell within the heart with unutterable glory. Sometimes it is a very quiet, simple consciousness, prompting one rather to walk by faith moment by moment, and abide in Christ in great simplicity for every instant's need; and there is no transcendent emotion, but simply a satisfying consciousness of Christ sufficient for our practical life. But in every case it is really satisfaction, and we know that the Lord has come to abide with us forever, and be our all-sufficiency, and our everlasting portion.

7. The Holy Spirit now begins to lead us in the steppings of a holy life. We find it is to be maintained by the moment. We have no crystalized and stereotyped condition of self-centered life, but we have Christ for the present moment, and must abide in Him by the moment. We must walk in the Spirit, and we shall not fulfill the lusts of the flesh. We must be filled with the Spirit, and we shall have no room for sin. It is now that we find the importance of walking in the Spirit, and maintaining steadfastly the habit of obedience and fellowship with Him as the essential condition of the life of holiness. One of the first and most important lessons is to hearken to His voice. The minding of the Spirit is life and peace, but the minding of the flesh is death. The Spirit is given, we are distinctly told, to them that obey Him; and the disobedient and inattentive heart will find His fellowship constantly liable to be interrupted and suspended. The life of holiness is

not a mere abstract state, but a mosaic, made up of a thousand minute details of life and action.

A Christian lady, while thinking of the subject of sanctification, found herself suddenly absorbed in a sort of waking vision, in which she seemed to see a builder erecting an edifice of stone. First, she saw a deep excavation, and at the bottom of it a solid rock on which the house was to be planted. Across this rock was written the name of Christ, with the words, "Other foundation can no man lay than that which is laid, which is Jesus Christ." Then a derrick swung before her eyes and a stone was deposited in the rear of the building. It was a very plain looking block of granite, with no decorations whatever on its face, and as it was deposited, in an obscure portion of the wall was the word "Humility." Next, the derrick swung around to the front of the wall and planted another foundation stone on the principal corner, and the name of this was "Faith." The walls now rose rapidly; block after block of enduring granite was planted and cemented, and at length was fashioned into a magnificent arch surrounded by a beautiful cornerstone, the most lovely stone in all the building, and across it was written the name, "Love" Between these principal stones the interstices were filled up with innumerable small pieces of every size and shape, and these were variously named by the qualities of the Christian character, such as meekness, gentleness, temperance, forbearance, patience, considerateness, serenity, courtesy, cheerfulness, etc., and then the whole facade was spanned by one glowing word in golden letters, "Sanctification." The prejudices of a lifetime were at once removed, and she saw the loveliness of a holy life and character, and the true meaning of the word that she had so long misconceived and disliked.

This, then, is the Holy Spirit's work in the life, and holiness; it is much more than a mere blank sheet of spotless white; it is the living portrait wrought out upon that sheet in all the lineaments of holy loveliness, and all the positive qualities of a practical and beautiful Christian life. "The fruit of the Spirit is love, joy, peace, longsuffering, gentleness, meekness, temperance, and faith," and "whatsoever things are just, whatsoever things are true, whatsoever things are pure, whatsoever things are honest, whatsoever things are lovely, whatsoever things are of good report, if there be any virtue, and if there be any praise, think on these things."

These things the Holy Spirit comes to transcribe in our hearts and to reflect in our lives, and yet these qualities are not our own, in any sense in which we could claim them as the result of our own goodness, or rest in them as permanent, personal attributes. They are rather to be regarded as the grace of Christ, supplied to us from His own indwelling Spirit moment by moment. "And of His fullness have all we received, and grace for grace." This is the grace to produce in us all the varied graces of the Christian life. As Peter expresses it, "We are called to show forth the excellencies of Christ," rather than our own, "who hath called us out of darkness into His marvelous light." These are the bridal robes which are granted to the Lamb's wife, "that she should be arrayed in raiment clean and white." These are like Rebecca's ornaments and veil, which are not woven by her hands, but brought her by Eleazar from Isaac himself, and which, she had simply to put on and wear as his gifts.

So, the Holy Ghost, typified by Abraham's servant, brings to us the wedding robe, and supplies to us day by day the special garment that fits us for each new situation and emergency, and we simply put on the Lord Jesus and walk in Him as our all-sufficiency for every place of duty and trial. The Spirit is ever present to reveal Him to us in every new aspect of grace and fullness; and every new need or failure is but an invitation to take Him in greater fullness, and prove in a higher sense that He is indeed able to save unto the uttermost, and to keep unto the end. Not only does the Holy Spirit thus lead us into the positive graces of the Christian life, but He also keeps us perpetually cleansed from all the stains of spiritual defilement, and even from the effects of temptation and evil suggestion. If sin should touch the heart but for a moment, He is there to reveal instantly the evil and in the same flash of light to present and apply a remedy. "And, if we walk in the light as He is in the light, the blood of Jesus Christ keeps cleansing us from all sin."

Thus the soul, like the pebble in the stream, lets in the perpetual cleansing of His life. Indeed, we may walk so close to Him that before the sin is even admitted, before the temptation has reached the citadel of the will and becomes our own act, it is repelled at the entrance, and does not become our sin. He has promised to keep us as the apple of His eye, and, even as the eyelash is so constructed in the delicate organism of the human body that the very approach of the smallest particle of dust causes it instantly to close and repel the intruding substance, so the gentle Holy Ghost instinctively guards the heart and conscience from willful sin. There is something, however, even in the presence of temptation, and the surrounding atmosphere of a sin-defiled world, that spreads a certain contagion around us, like the air in the infected hospital. And it is necessary, therefore, that even this should be constantly cleansed, even as the falling showers wash away the dust from the pavements and the trees, and purify the summer air. This the Holy Spirit is constantly doing, and diffusing through the sanctified heart the freshness and sweetness of the heavenly atmosphere.

We find, therefore, in the Old Testament types, a beautiful provision for the cleansing of the people, even from the touch of the dead, through the water of separation. (Numbers 19.) This beautiful ordinance was a type of the Holy Spirit applying to us the atonement of Christ, and cleansing us habitually from the very breath, and even the indirect contagion of surrounding evil. Even if our old, dead carnal nature touches us, or the atmosphere of sin is around us, we have constantly this water of separation, and the moment we are sprinkled with it every effect is removed and the spirit is quickened into freshness and sweetness, even as the waters that revive the famished earth, and cause the desert to blossom as the rose.

We must ever bear in mind, in tracing the Holy Spirit's work in the believer's heart, the distinction between purity of heart and maturity of character. From the moment that the soul is yielded to Christ in full surrender, and He is received as its divine and indwelling life, we have His purity, and the old, sinful self is reckoned dead, and in no sense recognized as our true self. There is a complete and eternal divorce, and the old heart is henceforth treated as if it were not, and Christ recognized as the true I, and, of course, a life that is essentially pure and divine. But, although wholly separated from the old, sinful life, is the new spirit yet in its infancy, and before it lie boundless stages of progress and development. The acorn is as complete in its parts as the oak of a thousand years, but not as fully developed. And so the soul which has just received Christ as its abiding life and sanctification, is as wholly sanctified, and as completely one with Him as Enoch or John is today, but not as mature. This is the meaning of Christian growth; we do not grow into holiness, we receive holiness in Christ as a complete, divine life; complete in all its parts from the beginning, and divine, as Christ is. But it is like the infant Christ on Mary's bosom, and it has to grow up into all the fullness of the stature of perfect manhood in Christ.

This is the work of the Holy Ghost, as the mother and the nurse, the teacher, educator, cherisher of our spiritual life, and it is in this connection that we must learn to walk in the Spirit, and rise with Him into "all the good pleasure of His goodness, and the work of faith with power," until we shall have reached the fullness of His own prayer for us. "Now the God of peace that brought again from the dead the Lord Jesus Christ, great Shepherd of the sheep, through the blood of the everlasting covenant, make you perfect in every good work to do His will, working in you that which is pleasing in His sight, through Jesus Christ; to whom be glory forever and ever. Amen."

Chapter 8: THE SPIRIT OF LIFE

Romans 8.

What is life? The unsolved question of science and philosophy. What is it that makes the difference between that soaring bird with buoyant wing and burnished breast, as it mounts the air, and that little limp, broken thing that the hunter gathers up in his hand a moment later, as it has fallen before the cruel fire? What is the cause of this strange, terrible change? The galvanic battery can mimic some of the movements of life in muscle and limb, but when the current ceases the movement stops, and in a few hours the flesh has yielded to the power of corruption, and is dissolving into earth again.

What life does, we know, but what it is, science marks with a note of interrogation.

One of the most remarkable popular books of science, from a Christian standpoint, is Professor Drummond's "Natural Law in the Spiritual World," but perhaps the only thoroughly weak and unsatisfactory chapter in it is that in which he tries to define life and death.

Science is approaching slowly the true center which the Bible gave us so long ago. It is steadily reducing all vital force to one essential principle, perhaps electricity. The Bible has settled the question long ago in regard to Him who is the source of life: "This is the true God and eternal life." God is the fount of life, and Christ is the life of God for men, and His life is the true source of life for the souls and bodies of His children. This life He imparts to us through the Holy Spirit, who becomes to the soul that is united to Him, the medium and the channel of vital union and communion with Christ, our Living Head. It is thus that the Holy Spirit is the Spirit of life in Christ Jesus, because He imparts to us the life of Jesus. It is especially of His part, in connection with our physical life, that we are to speak at this time.

That He should be able to quicken our mortal bodies should not seem strange even upon the most general view of the subject. As we have already intimated, even physical science has been learning, in some measure, to recognize life, not so much as a matter of external organism and coarse material elements, as of vital force.

Half a century has changed radically the methods of treatment known to medical science, and led physicians to rely much more upon natural forces and resources, and more subtle and vital elements, to counteract the power of disease than formerly.

The influence of air and occupation, of surrounding circumstances and mental conditions, all these have far greater weight today than formerly, because health is recognized as the result of inward forces more than of outward agencies. These are distinct approximations toward the higher truth, that the source of our strength must be looked for in the direct power and contact of that spiritual personality in whom "we live, and move, and have our being."

This is the plain teaching of the Holy Scriptures from beginning to end, and we shall probably be surprised to find how much is taught in these sacred pages respecting the relation of the Holy Spirit to our physical life.

I. The Part of the Holy Spirit in Creation.

We know that the Divine Spirit is recognized in the Scriptures as the direct agent in the original creation, and the Spirit of life and order in the whole domain in nature and providence.

How strikingly all this is described in the majestic Psalm of nature, the one hundred and fourth: "Thou hidest Thy face, they are troubled; Thou takest away their breath, they die, and return to their dust. Thou sendest forth Thy Spirit, they are created; and Thou renewest the face of the earth."

This is, however, the power that formed the heavens with their orbs of light, that covers the woods and fields with their robes of many-tinted glory, that animates the teeming world of insect and animal life, that breathed into man the breath of life at the beginning, and still sustains his physical existence, and that has created all his mortal powers and endowments. Why should it be thought strange that He who made us should sustain us, restore us, and "quicken our mortal bodies by His Spirit that dwelleth in us?"

II. The Work of the Holy Spirit in the Body in the Old Testament.

We have a very remarkable pattern of physical life in one of the Old Testament biographies. It is the story of Samson, and it was directly intended as a lesson of the true nature and source of physical strength.

Samson's stupendous power was not due to physical organization at all, but only and directly to the power and presence of the Holy Spirit, for in the very beginning of his strength it is repeatedly added, that "the Spirit of the Lord began to move him, the Spirit of the Lord came upon him," etc. Judges 12: 25; 14: 6; 14: 19; and 16: 28.

When he was deserted by the Holy Spirit he was helpless in the hands of his enemies, but when he was filled with the superhuman power of God's Spirit he could carry away the gates of the city, or hurl the walls of Dagon's temple upon the assembled thousands of his enemies.

The lesson of his life is unmistakably foreshadowed in the great New Testament truth that our bodily life as well as our spiritual has its root and nourishment in God, and that, as we walk in separation from evil, and fellowship with Him, "He that raised up Jesus from the dead will also quicken our mortal bodies by the Spirit that dwelleth in us."

III. The Part of the Holy Spirit in the Personal Ministry of Christ.

It was He that wrought the supernatural works of the Lord Jesus on earth. Not one miracle did he perform until He received the baptism of the Holy Ghost. Then he said, "The Spirit of the Lord is upon me, for He hath sent me to heal the brokenhearted, to set at liberty them that are bruised;"

and when his enemies attributed his miracles to the power of Satan, He distinctly declared that they were performed by the power of the Holy Ghost, and added, "If I by the Holy Ghost cast out devils, no doubt the kingdom of God has come unto you." And then he proceeded to charge them with the fatal sin against the Holy Ghost in thus attributing His works to Satan. See Matt. 12: 28.

If then, Christ cast out demons and wrought miracles by the power of the Holy Ghost, and it is the same Spirit who still abides in the church, and dwells in the hearts and bodies of believers, why should it be thought strange that the Almighty Spirit, who thus wrought in the Son of God, should work in our bodies the same works, and thus quicken them, as our text declares?

IV. The Part of the Holy Ghost in the Apostolic Ministry,

and in the Permanent Enduement of the Church.

It was not until the Holy Spirit descended that the apostles were permitted to exercise their ministry in power, and all the mighty works that followed are distinctly attributed by Peter and the other apostles to His personal working. He quotes from the prophet Joel the distinct promise, "I will pour out in those days of my Spirit," and it is followed by the announcement that shall ensue, "And I will show wonders in the heavens above, and miracles in the earth beneath."

It was after the Holy Ghost descended again, a little later, until the place was shaken, that we read, "By the hands of the apostles were many signs and wonders wrought among the people." And it was to be through His continuance and supernatural presence that the divine gifts were to be manifested in the church to the end of the dispensation. 1 Cor. 12: 4. "There are diversities of gifts, but the same Spirit. To one there is given the word of wisdom; to another the word of knowledge by the same Spirit, to another faith by the same Spirit, to another the gifts of healing by the same Spirit, to another the working of miracles by the same Spirit, but all these worketh that one and the self-same Spirit, dividing to everyone severally as he will."

Thus we see that all the supernatural effects of Christianity are accomplished through the Holy Spirit. It is His very province to perpetuate in the Church the very works that Christ performed through Him on earth, the Church being simply the body of the ascended Savior, and the channel through which He is to work in the same divine manner; even as the Master said when promising His coming: "The works that I do shall he do also; and greater works than these he shall do, because I go to my Father."

Why then, should it seem strange that this blessed Spirit should do the very work He came to do, and still quicken our mortal bodies as He dwells within us?

V. The Special Ministry of the Holy Ghost for our Bodies.

In the sixth chapter of 1 Corinthians, the dignity and sacredness of the human body are very clearly presented as an argument against impurity in our social relations. "Know ye not," He asks, "that your bodies are the members of Christ?" verse 15; and then, verse 19, "What! know ye not that your body is the temple of the Holy Ghost?" Previously, in this epistle, He had spoken of the Spirit's ministry within us in a more spiritual sense -- chapter 3: 16, 17 -- but here

He refers explicitly to His union with our physical life, and with the body of Jesus Christ as God's substitute for unholy physical connection. The body is for the Lord and the Lord for the body; and it is the ministry of the Holy Ghost thus to unite our body to our Lord's, and to inhabit it and hold it in sacredness and purity for Him.

Let us distinctly understand that it is of our physical life that these Scriptures speak, not our spiritual. That is also united to Christ. But surely with so much teaching regarding that portion of our being, we can afford to claim these specific references for that which was intended by them - - our consecrated physical life.

The only way in which the simple and conclusive effect of our text can be turned aside is by attempting to apply it to the future resurrection, as sometimes has been done. It is therefore well that we should carefully look at its connection, and establish its true application on sound exegetical grounds.

1. The general connection of the whole chapter makes this very plain. No less an authority than John Calvin has proved that this passage cannot refer to the future resurrection, because the apostle is speaking, in this place, of the present work of the Holy Ghost in the believer, and it is not until much later that he advances to the future hopes that await us at the Lord's coming, which he does enlarge upon after the eighteenth verse. The subject of the chapter is the blessed indwelling of the Holy Spirit in those who have yielded themselves wholly to Christ.

The first effect of His indwelling is given in the second verse; it is deliverance from indwelling sin through the indwelling of the Holy Ghost.

The second is the new habit of obedience to the Spirit, expressed so beautifully in the eighth chapter of Romans, fifth and sixth verses, by the expression, "The minding of the Spirit is life and peace." "They that after the Spirit do mind the things of the Spirit."

The third effect of the Spirit's indwelling is His quickening life for our bodies, and this is here described in the text.

In the previous verse the body is recognized as well as the soul, as yielded up to death, and so reckoned as good as dead, that we do not henceforth depend upon its natural strength as sufficient; but in contrast with this the Holy Spirit becomes its new life and quickens our mortal body by the same power which raised Christ from the dead.

This follows later in the chapter, verses 14, 15.

The blessed leading of the Holy Ghost through the experience of Christian life, culminating at last in the realization of our future hope when we shall enter into the full redemption of the body at Christ's second coming, verse 23; but even of this full redemption of the body, we are told in the same verse, that we have even now the first fruits of the Spirit. That is, of course, the quickening influence which the Spirit exercises, even in the present life, in our mortal bodies, and which is the foretaste of the full resurrection.

Thus, the very order of the chapter prepares us to apply the text to a present experience. John Calvin, as we have already stated, does so, but instead of recognizing that present Spirit as divine healing, of which probably the good reformer never thought, He regards it as the consecrating of our bodies to the service and glory of God, a sense, of course, which the word quicken does not bear.

2. This leads us to inquire into the meaning of the word "quicken."

It would require a very strong inversion, and, we almost think, perversion of the word, to apply this term to the consecration of the body, for it literally means the reviving, stimulating, animating, invigorating of its strength.

The nearest parallel passage where it is employed is in this same epistle, a few chapters previously, where it is applied, chapter 4: 17, to the act which God performed in quickening the body of Abraham when he was past age, and also the vital organs of Sarah, his wife, so that Isaac was born contrary to nature.

In this case, neither Abraham nor Sarah were dead, but their vital system was exhausted, and it was simply quickened, revived and renewed.

Thus the word would not suggest the literal resurrection of the dead, but rather the reviving and restoring of strength when it is exhausted; precisely what is done when our failing health is renewed, and our infirmities are healed by the indwelling power of the Holy Spirit through the name of Jesus.

3. It will make this conclusion still more obvious if we remember that it is our mortal bodies that are here described, not our souls at all, but our physical organization.

This, therefore, is a direct operation of the Holy Spirit upon our vital functions, organs and health, and any other application is contrary to the simple and natural meaning of the passage.

4. That this is not the resurrection body is certain from the fact that it is called the mortal body. Now the mortal body means a dying body, and certainly that is not a dead body, and still more certainly, it is not a resurrected body, for the bodies of the saints, when raised from the dead at Christ's coming, shall not be mortal bodies, but immortal, nor "can they die any more," our Lord Himself has said.

5. The whole induction of proof is crowned by the clause "that dwelleth in us."

Now that must mean the present dwelling of the Holy Spirit in our present mortal bodies. It cannot mean our buried dust, for then the Spirit will not be dwelling in us. It is a process which is now going on through the present indwelling and inworking of the Holy Ghost.

We might add to these thoughts the impressive one suggested by the terms, "the Spirit of Him that raised up Jesus from the dead." This is the Spirit of a physical resurrection. The resurrection of Christ from the dead was a spiritual resurrection. His soul was not dead, it was His body that was raised from the tomb, and if it be the pattern of the Spirit's working in us in this connection, it must have reference to our body too.

We have not sufficiently realized the physical meaning of Christ's resurrection, or given due weight to the stupendous fact that He who came forth from that grave has become the physical head of our life, and that "we are members of His body, His flesh, and of His bones," and have a right to draw from His glorious frame the fullness of His life and strength, so far as these vessels of clay can hold it and use it for His service and glory.

Thus we see that the Holy Spirit has a direct ministry for our bodies, even as Christ's body has a direct relation to our physical being. Have we thus received Him? Do we thus know Him? And, ceasing to depend upon our natural strength, have we learned the blessed secret, "He giveth power to the faint; and to them that have no might He increaseth strength." "They that wait upon the Lord shall change their strength; they shall mount up with wings as eagles; they shall run and not be weary, they shall walk and not faint."

VI. The Relation of the Holy Spirit to the Future Resurrection.

This is the climax of the simple argument respecting the blessed working of the Holy Spirit in our bodies.

While he quickens our mortal bodies now, there is awaiting us a glorious and immortal tabernacle which shall be fashioned like unto the body of His glory.

Speaking of it, the apostle says, "For we know that if our earthly house of this tabernacle were dissolved, we have a building of God, an house not made with hands, eternal in the heavens. For in this we groan, earnestly desiring to be clothed upon with our house which is from heaven; if so be that being clothed we shall not be found naked. For we that are in this tabernacle do groan, being burdened; not for that we would be unclothed, but clothed upon, that mortality might be swallowed up of life." And then he adds, "Now He that hath wrought us for the self-same thing is God," that is for the physical resurrection. And then follows this most important sentence which should be perfectly weighed, "who also hath given unto us the earnest of the Spirit."

Anyone who knows the meaning of the word "earnest" need not have it demonstrated that it implies the first sample in actual kind of the flower and fruit which is afterwards to follow.

An earnest of the harvest is the first sheaf, the very same in kind as that which is to come. An earnest of the field produced, is a handful of the very soil which we have bought. And so, an earnest of the resurrection is a part of that resurrection life experienced now in our physical frame.

To say that the Holy Spirit in our hearts is the earnest, would be to contradict the very meaning of the terms, to make a thing of a different class, an earnest of something utterly diverse. The Spirit in our hearts now is an earnest of our spiritual exaltation yonder, the Spirit in our mortal bodies now is an earnest of the resurrection of the body then in physical immortality.

This is exactly what the apostle said in parallel passage, Rom. 8: 23, "We ourselves, which have the firstfruits of the Spirit, even we ourselves groan within ourselves, waiting for the adoption, to wit, the redemption of our body."

We have the firstfruits of the resurrection, and we are waiting for the full harvest, and the firstfruits are, verse 11, "If the Spirit of Him that raised up Jesus from the dead dwell in you, he that raised up Christ from the dead shall also quicken your mortal bodies by his Spirit that dwelleth in you."

We have all we can hold in the vessel of clay now; we shall then have all we can contain in the larger vessel of glory, when, thrilled with the rapturous touch of His life, we shall soar away from the fetters of the tomb and the restraints of our present frailties and limitations, into all the might and majesty of His own glorious life and power. Then, like Him, our flesh shall be "like fine brass, as if it burned in a furnace, our eyes like flames of fire," our bodies able to penetrate through material barriers, to rise beyond the clouds, to spurn the restraining forces of matter and nature, to possess immeasurable space, and share his own divine and mighty works; for we shall be like Him when we see Him as He is.

But this we may have even now in foretaste, as the Spirit quickens our mortal bodies, until we take hold of the glory of the resurrection.

In Conclusion.

How shall we walk in this Spirit of life?

1. We must have Him as the occupant of our heart; we must know Him by a deep and real spiritual experience. Everything in its own order; and the new order is, first, the spiritual and then the material.

Like Him who came from the innermost shrine of the tabernacle, moving outward to meet His people, so the Holy Ghost still comes from the holy place to the heart until He fills all the extremities of our physical being, so that divine healing has been called the overflow of the Holy Ghost from a heart that can hold no more, and pours its redundant fullness into every open channel of our physical life.

2. We must distinctly recognize the promise of His residence in our bodies, and claim Him in this specific way. Every new experience must first be apprehended and then appropriated; and so we must see them to be a redemption right, and then put forth our hand and take of the Tree of Life and eat and live forever.

3. We must receive the Holy Ghost as an abiding guest into our flesh as well as our heart.

The word dwell, translated, in this verse, is a very strong one. It is the Greek word 'oikeo,' and in the last clause the still stronger expression, 'enoikeo.' It means to dwell habitually; to dwell as we dwell at home, to be the welcome, constant guest, and find His residence not only with us, but, as the last term expresses, in the innermost depths of our being.

4. We must abide in Him by hearkening to His voice, obeying His will, using our strength for His service and glory, and constantly recognizing Him, and not mere natural strength, as the source of our life.

This habit can be cultivated; God may have to train us in it by cutting off the outward supplies and sources of physical power; He may let the natural life wither until it seems we must sink and die, and, as stated in the previous verse, if Christ be in us the body is dead because of sin, but then we must remember that the Spirit is life because of righteousness. And though, like Paul in 2 Cor. 4: 11, we seem to be almost delivered unto death for Jesus' sake, yet we must receive the life of Christ in our mortal flesh, and we shall find that it is still as true as it was in Paran's desert and Judah's wilderness, that "man must not live by bread alone, but by every word that proceedeth out of the mouth of God."

Chapter 9: THE SPIRIT OF COMFORT

"Walking in the comfort of the Holy Ghost." Acts 9: 31.

Our English translators have given to the Greek work 'Paraclete,' which the Lord Jesus applied to the Holy Ghost, the translation of the Comforter. And while this term is not expressive of the complete sense of the original, yet it expresses very beautifully one of the most blessed characters and offices of the Holy Spirit.

I. He is the author of peace.

It is twofold peace, peace with God and the peace of God. We find many references to this twofold rest. "Come unto me all ye that labor and are heavy laden and I will give you rest." This is the rest which the troubled soul receives when it comes to Christ for pardon. But then there is a deeper rest: "Take my yoke upon you and learn of me who am meek and lowly in heart, and ye shall find rest unto your souls." This is experienced after the surrender of the will to God, and the discipline of the Spirit fully received. So again the prophet Isaiah announces, "Thou wilt keep him in perfect peace, whose mind is stayed on thee."

John 20:22

There is a deeper peace, so we find the risen Savior meeting the disciples in the upper room with the salutation. "Peace be unto you," as He shows them His hands and His side; but later, He breathes on them and adds a second benediction of peace as they receive the Holy Ghost. Peace with God is the effect of forgiveness. "Therefore being justified by faith, we have peace with God through our Lord Jesus Christ." This is the gift of the Holy Spirit as He seals upon the heart the assurance of God's pardoning work, and breathes the witness of acceptance. And yet this is dependent upon our believing and resting in the promise. We must cooperate with the Holy Spirit. He witnesses 'with' our spirit, not 'to' our spirit, that we are the children of God. "In whom also, after that ye believed, ye were sealed with that Holy Spirit of promise." "The God of hope fill you with all joy and peace in believing that ye may abound in hope by the power of the Holy Ghost." Thus we see that we must cooperate in believing.

Rom 8:16

The peace of God is a deeper experience; it comes from the indwelling of God Himself in the heart that has been surrendered wholly to Him, and it is nothing less than the very heart of Christ resting in our heart, possessing our Spirit, and imparting to us the very same peace which He manifested even in that awful hour when all others were filled with dismay, but He was calm and victorious, even in the prospect of the garden and the cross. It is the deep, tranquil, eternal rest of God, taking the place of the restless, troubled sea of our own thoughts, fears and agitations. It is the very peace of God, and it passeth all understanding, and keeps the heart and mind through Christ Jesus our Lord. It is the special gift of the Holy Ghost; nay, it is rather His own personal abiding, as the Dove of Rest, spreading His tranquil wings over the troubled sea of human strife and passion, and bringing His own everlasting rest.

Have we entered into His rest, and are we walking with Him in the secret place of the Most High? What gift is more necessary and delightful in this world of disquiet and change? What would the world not give for an opiate that could charm away its cares and fears, and lull its heart to such divine repose; and yet from the Paraclete of love, and the brooding wing of the holy Dove, men refuse the gift for which their hearts are breaking, and their lives are wearing out in the fret and friction of strife and sin. This is the true element of spiritual growth and power. "In quietness and confidence shall be your strength," is the mission of the very Comforter to bring. "Let us, therefore, fear lest a promise being left us of entering into His rest, any of you would seem to come short of it. Let us labor, therefore, to enter into this rest lest any of you should fail after the same example of unbelief."

II. The Spirit of Joy.

This is a deeper and fuller spring, but the source is the same, the bosom of the Comforter. The kingdom of God, we are told, is not meat and drink, but righteousness and peace, and joy in the Holy Ghost. This also is the joy of Christ Himself. It is the Spirit's business to take the things that are Christ's and reveal them to us. And so the Master has said, "These things have I said unto you, that my joy might remain in you, and that your joy might be full." "Hitherto have ye asked nothing in my name; ask and ye shall receive that your joy may be full." We have some conception of His joy. Even in the dark and dreadful hour when the powers of darkness were gathering about Him for the final struggle, and even His Father's face was about to be covered with the awful cloud of desertion and judgment, still he could rise superior to His surroundings and so forget His own troubles as to think only of His disciples and say to them, "Let not your heart be troubled."

Like the martyrs, afterwards, at the stake and amid the flames, who testified that so deep was their inward joy that they were unconscious of external agony, so He was transported above His anguish by the very joy of His Father's presence and love. It was this that enabled Him to endure, "for the joy set before Him He endured the cross, despising the shame." He saw not the deep, dark valley of humiliation, but the heights of resurrection-life and ascension-glory just beyond; and He was lifted above the consciousness of the present by the vision of hope, and the joy of the Lord. This is the joy He will give to us. It is nothing less than the fullness of His own heart throbbing in our breast and sharing with us His own immutable blessedness.

Therefore, this joy is wholly independent of surrounding circumstances of natural temperament. It is not a spirit of native cheerfulness, but it is a perennial fountain of divine gladness, springing up from sources that lie far below the soil of human nature. It is the same anointing of which the prophet said of Christ Himself, "Thy God hath anointed thee with the oil of gladness above thy fellows."

Now this divine joy is the privilege of all consecrated believers. We need it for victory in the trying places of life. "The joy of the Lord is your strength." Satan always takes special advantage of a depressed and discouraged heart. Victory must be won in the conflict by a spirit of gladness and praise. The hosts of God must march into the battle with songs of rejoicing. The world must see the light of heaven in our faces if it would believe in the reality of our religion.

Therefore, we find the Scriptures exhorting us to "rejoice in the Lord always, and in everything give thanks, for this is the will of God in Christ Jesus concerning us." But the secret of such a love must be a heart possessed and overflowing with the Holy Ghost. "The fruit of the Spirit is love, joy and peace." We cannot find these springs in the soil of time, they flow from the throne of God and of the Lamb. But a soul that dwells in the innermost shrine of the Master's presence will ever know it and reflect it. It can no more be concealed than the sunshine of heaven, and it will light up the humblest life and the most trying situation, just as the sun itself lights up the lowly cabin, and shines through the dark vault, if only it can find an opening where it may enter in. Are you walking in the light of the Lord and filled with His joy? And can we sing:

God is the treasure of my soul,

A source of lasting joy;

A joy which want cannot impair

Nor death itself destroy?

III. The Spirit of Comfort and Consolation.

It is especially in the hour of distress and trial that the Comforter becomes manifest in His peculiar ministry of consolation and love. It is then that the promise is fulfilled which applies more especially to this person of the Godhead as the very Mother of the soul. "As one whom his mother comforteth, so will I comfort you; and ye shall be comforted in Jerusalem."

1. Comfort implies the existence of trial; and the happiest life is not the one freest from affliction, but they who walk in the Spirit will always be found familiar with the paths of sorrow and the adverse circumstances of life. Nowhere are the followers of the Man of Sorrows promised exemption from the fellowship of His sufferings, but every element of blessing they possess carries with it an added source of trial. To them the world is less a home than to its own children, and their dearest friends are the readiest to misunderstand their lives and cross their wishes. To them comes the experience of temptation and spiritual conflict, as it does not come to the worldling and the sinner, and they have often cause to feel and know

"The path of sorrow and that path alone,

Leads to the land where sorrow is unknown.

No traveler ever reached that blessed abode,

Who found not thorns and briers in the road."

But all these are but occasions to prove the love and faithfulness of God. The storm cloud is but the background for the rainbow, and the falling tear but an occasion for the gentle hand of the Comforter to wipe it away.

2. The comfort is in proportion to the trial. There is a blessed equilibrium of joy and sorrow. As the sufferings of Christ abound in us, so our consolation also abounds in Christ. As far as the pendulum swings backward, so far it swings forward. Every trial is, therefore, a prophecy of blessing to the heart that walks with Jesus. A dear saint of God once remarked, near the close of life, "God has seemed all my life to be so sorry for the trials He gave me in the beginning, that He has been trying to make up for it ever since." This is a blessed compensation even here, and by-and-by we shall find that "our light affliction, which was but for a moment, worketh for us a far more exceeding, even an eternal weight of glory."

3. Times of trial are, therefore, often our times of greatest joy. God's nightingales sing at midnight, and

Sorrow touched by God grows bright

With more than rapturous ray,

As darkness shows us worlds of light

We never saw by day.

It was when the apostles were turned out of Antioch by a mob of respectable men and honorable women, that the record was added, "The disciples were filled with joy and with the Holy Ghost." It was when the fig-tree refused to blossom, and the vines were stripped of their accustomed fruit, and nature was robed in a winding sheet of death, that Habakkuk's song rose to its highest notes of triumph, and he could say "Yet I will rejoice in the Lord, and glory in the God of my salvation." There is such a thing as "sorrowful yet always rejoicing;" a bitter sweet which draws its quintessence of joy from the very wormwood and the gall, and which knows not whether to weep or sing as it cries, with Pascal, in the one breath "joy upon joy, tears upon tears!"

Oh! it is a blessed testimony to the grace of God and the Spirit's abundant love, when we can rise above our circumstances and "count it all joy, even when we fall into diverse temptations," and "rejoice, inasmuch as we are partakers of the sufferings of Christ, because when His glory shall be revealed we shall be glad with exceeding joy."

4. If we would know the full comfort of the Holy Spirit we must cooperate with Him, and rejoice by simple faith, often when our circumstances are all forbidding, and even our very feelings give no response of sympathy or conscious joy. It is a great thing to learn to 'count it' all joy. Counting is not the language of poetry or sentiment, but of cold, unerring calculation. It adds up the column thus: sorrow, temptation, difficulty, opposition, depression, desertion, danger, discouragement on every side, but at the bottom of the column God's presence, God's will, God's joy, God's promise, God's recompense. "Our light affliction, which is but for a moment, worketh for us a far more exceeding, even an eternal weight of glory." How much does the column amount to? Lo! the sum of all the addition is "ALL JOY," for "the sufferings of this present time are not worthy to be compared with the glory to be revealed."

That is the way to count your joy. Singly, a given circumstance may not seem joyful, but counted in with God, and His presence and promise, it makes a glorious sum in the arithmetic of faith. We can rejoice in the Lord as an act of will, and when we do, the Comforter will soon bring all our emotions into line, yea, and all our circumstances too. They who went into battle with songs of praise in front soon had songs of praise in the rear, and an abundant, visible cause of thanksgiving. Therefore, let us say with the apostle, "I do rejoice, yea, and I will rejoice."

5. The Holy Spirit's joys and consolations are administered to the heart in His infinite and sovereign wisdom, according to His purpose, for our spiritual training, and with reference to our spiritual state, or our immediate needs and prospects. Frequently, He sends His sweetest whispers as the reward of special obedience in some difficult and trying place. Not only at the judgment, but now also does the Master say, "Well done, good and faithful servant, enter into the joy of thy Lord." That joy is experienced here, and the good and faithful servant has the recompense of special service and obedience in the place of difficulty and testing.

Matt 25.

Sometimes, again, the Spirit's comforts are sent to prepare us for some impending hour of trial, that when the storm bursts upon us we may remember the Master's love, and be cheered and sustained through the trying hour, even as the Holy Spirit came on Jordan's banks, and the Father's voice just before the forty days of dark, fierce temptation. Sometimes, again, the Spirit's love-tokens come just after some dark and terrible conflict, even as the angels appeared after Gethsemane to comfort our weary and suffering Lord. Sometimes, also, His comforts are withdrawn to keep us from leaning too strongly on sensible joys, and to discipline us in the life of simple faith, and teach us to trust when we cannot see the face of our Beloved, or hear the music of His voice.

6. But we must ever remember, in connection with our varied experiences, that even comfort and joy are not to be the aim and goal of our hearts, but rather that the principle of our Christian life is simple faith, and the purpose, faithful obedience and service to our Master.

"Not enjoyment and not sorrow

Is our destined end and way;

But to act that each tomorrow

Finds us farther than today."

The life that is naturally influenced by sunshine or shadow will be ephemeral, and change its hue like the chameleon, with the seasons and surroundings. Indeed, the very source of lasting joy is to ignore our own emotions and feelings and act uniformly on the twin principles of faith and duty. Many people are trying to get joyful emotions just as they would buy cut flowers in winter. They are bright and fragrant for a few hours, but they have no root, and they wither away with the sunset. Far better and wiser to plant the root in the fertile ground, to water it, and to wait for it, and in a little while the lasting blossoms will open their petals and breathe out their fragrance on the air. So the joy that springs from trust and permanent spiritual life is as abiding as its source.

Let us, therefore, learn to ignore the immediate impressions that lie upon the surface of our consciousness, and steadfastly walk in the fellowship and will of the Divine Spirit, and thus there shall grow in our hearts and lives the roots of happiness and all their blessed fruits of joy and consolation. Often, therefore, has God to withdraw, for a time, the conscious joy, that He may prove us and develop in us the faith that trusts Him, and loves Him for Himself, rather than for the sweetest of His gifts.

A dear friend once came to us complaining that her spiritual joy had all left her, and that her heart was like a stone. There seemed no disobedience in her life, and no defect in her faith, and we could only commit her to the Master for all the teaching she might need. A few days afterwards she came with radiant countenance to tell how it had all ended. "The darkness," she said, "continued until I told the Lord that if He wanted me to be willing to trust Him in the dark, and to bear this for Him, I would do so as long as He was pleased to continue it. The moment I had yielded my will and accepted His, the dawn of heaven burst upon my soul, and the light returned with more than its former gladness, and I knew that He had only been testing me to teach me to trust Him for His own dear sake, and to walk by faith and not by sight."

Thus, let us delight ourselves in the Lord, and He will give us the desires of our heart. Let us aim supremely to please and glorify Him, and we shall find that "to glorify God" is "to enjoy Him forever." Let us rise above even the joy of the Lord to the Lord Himself, and having Him, it shall be forever true of us, "I will see you again, and your heart shall rejoice, and your joy, no man taketh from you." "My joy shall remain in you and your joy shall be full." "Thy sun shall no more go down, nor thy moon withdraw its shining, for the Lord shall be thine everlasting light, and thy days of mourning shall be ended."

Chapter 10: THE SPIRIT OF LOVE

"Walk in love." Eph. 5: 2.

"The fruit of the Spirit is love." Gal 5: 22.

The legend has come to us that when the apostle John was old, and waiting for His Master's call, he used to rise in the pulpit of the church in Ephesus each Lord's Day, as it came, and looking tenderly in the faces of the assembled people, simply say, "Little children, love one another," and sit down. And when the brethren asked him why he said nothing else, he simply answered, "There is nothing else to say; that is all there is, for, He that dwelleth in love dwelleth in God, and God in him."

Certainly, both Christ and His apostles have given to love, at least, the supreme, if not the exclusive place in the circle of Christian graces. It was the new commandment which Christ left with His disciples, and to which John exclusively refers in his epistle, when he says, His commandments are not grievous, and this is His commandment, that we should believe in the name of His Son Jesus Christ, and love one another, as He gave us commandment. Paul also declares, "Love is the fulfilling of the law;" therefore, he that loveth another hath fulfilled the law. And Christ Himself has declared that the whole law is fulfilled in one word, even in this: "Thou shalt love thy neighbor as thyself."

Someone has beautifully analyzed the fruit of the Spirit in Gal. 5: 22, and shown that all the graces there mentioned are but various forms of love itself. The apostle is not speaking of different fruits, but of one fruit, the fruit of the Spirit, and the various words that follow are but phrases and descriptions of the one fruit, which is love itself. Joy, which is first mentioned, is love on wings; peace, which follows, is love folding its wings, and nestling under the wings of God; longsuffering is love enduring; gentleness is love in society; goodness is love in activity, faith is love confiding; meekness is love stooping; temperance is true self-love, and the proper regard for our own real interests, which is as much the duty of love, as regard for the interests of others. Thus we see that love is essential to our whole Christian character, and indeed is the complement and crown of all else.

In the catalogue of spiritual gifts described by Paul in 1 Corinthians, it is named as preeminent to all the gifts of power, and the more excellent way than any enduement even of miraculous working or transcendent wisdom, without which all else will make us but as "sounding brass and a tinkling cymbal."

In the investiture of holy character, described by the apostle in Colossians, after all the old habiliments have been laid aside and the new robes of sanctity been put on, over all the rest we are invited to put on love, which is "the perfect bond" that is the girdle which holds all the other garments in their place and keeps them from falling off. And so, a soul without love must lose even the chief advantage of all other gifts, and faith and service be rendered ineffectual for lack of love. Therefore, it is the chief ministry of the Holy Spirit to teach us this heavenly lesson. In doing this

1. We must learn from Him that love is not a natural quality, but a direct gift of divine grace. The very word for love is charity, or 'caritas,' and this is derived from the root 'charis,' grace. So that the primary idea conveyed by the Bible term for love is, that it is a gift and not a natural quality. There is much earth-born love, and it would be narrow and blind to ignore the human virtues which have adorned the annals of history. The exquisite instinct of maternal love, the tender affection of the husband and wife, the brother and friend, the many refinements and amiabilities of the human character, the devotion of the patriot to his country, and the philanthropist to his kind -- these are holy affections which we would not, and do not, need to ignore. But human love has its limitations.

The love which the Holy Ghost teaches is not confined to any class or condition, but, like the love of God Himself, is able to reach and embrace not only the stranger and the alien, but also the unworthy, the unlovely, the unloving, and even the most malignant enemy and the most uncongenial object. It is nothing less than the very heart of God Himself infused into our heart. It is the love of God Himself imparted to us through the Holy Ghost. We cannot wring it out of our selfish hearts, or work it up by any effort of our will; it must come down to us from the very heart of God, and be shed abroad by the Holy Ghost Himself. This delightful fact makes the exercise of love a possibility for even the coldest and hardest heart. If it is a gift of grace, then it is available for all, and we have but to realize our need, yield ourselves unreservedly to God, be willing to receive it and exercise it and then claim it, and go forth to fulfill it in His strength. And as it is a gift, it involves no merit on the part of the receiver, for it is not our love, but the grace of our Lord Jesus Christ, to whom must ever be all the glory.

2. The love of God must be founded, like every other spiritual grace, on the exercise of faith. The apostle John, who understood this subject better than any other, gives the simple philosophy of love in these words, "We love Him because He first loved us;" and "we have known and believed the love that God hath to us." We must believe without wavering in God's personal love to us

before we can love Him in return. A single doubt in the heart respecting this will cloud the whole heavens. The spirit of implicit confidence in God will always lead to a spirit of filial love; and if we love Him that begetteth, we shall also love them that are begotten of Him.

Faith is, indeed, the channel of all spiritual blessings; hence the apostle Peter has said, "Add to your faith virtue, knowledge, temperance, and all the other graces." Hence, also, the apostles, when Christ was enjoining upon them the height and depth to which the forgiveness of injuries should extend, exclaimed, "Lord, increase our faith." They did not say, increase our love, for they seemed to have learned that if they had the faith which they should possess, they would inevitably possess the love. This is true. The fountain of love will always spring to the same height as the head-waters of faith have reached.

3. In order to receive this heavenly gift, the soul must be wholly surrendered to Christ, and receive the Holy Spirit as an abiding presence to bring into the heart the life of Jesus Christ, and to write the law of love upon the heart according to the terms of the new covenant. "I will write my law upon their hearts," is the promise of this new covenant, and put it into their inward part." This law is nothing but love, for love is the substance of the law, and the Holy Spirit came on the day of Pentecost, the anniversary of the law, as the spirit of power and obedience.

We enter into this new covenant, therefore, when we receive the Holy Spirit as our personal life, and indwelling guide and strength. And He brings into our spirit the abiding presence of Jesus Christ, uniting us to His person in such an intimate and perfect manner that we receive His very life into our own, and love in His love, and live in His very being. In order to do this there must, of course, be a renunciation of our own life and will, and the complete consecration of ourselves to Him. Then we receive Christ to abide, and all our life henceforth is through the virtue of His abiding union with us. This is the true secret of divine love.

A distinguished French evangelist was converted to God by preaching on the text, "Thou shalt love the Lord thy God with all thy heart, and soul, and mind, and strength." And finding, as he preached, his own inability to meet the demands of love, he was forced to fall back, even while preaching, upon the Lord Jesus Christ to meet his helplessness, and publicly acknowledge to the people that there was one way alone through which he could have help to obey this supreme law, the grace of the Lord Jesus Christ. In short, the secret of love is the same as all other graces, "Not I, but Christ that liveth in me." And this is what He is waiting to do for every willing heart.

4. But it is in the exercise of love in our practical Christian life that our chief lessons in walking with the Spirit must be learned, as our heavenly Teacher leads us in detail through the blessed, yet often painful discipline of the school of experience, and grounds us not only in the principles, but in the most difficult practice of this heavenly grace. One of His most frequent leadings is to bring us into a situation where we are required to exercise a love which we do not ourselves possess. We are confronted with circumstances which sorely test our spirit. Perhaps somewhere unkindness is allowed to be done to us, or we are associated with persons most uncongenial and disagreeable to us, or we hear of some trial that is before an enemy and are strongly tempted to conclude that they deserve the affliction, and are only suffering the judgment which they have brought upon themselves, when, on the contrary, the Holy Spirit is simply teaching us not to judge them at all, or even think a thought of condemnation, but rather pray for them and get our victory of love.

And yet, it is not in us to do this; our selfishness or pride leaps to the front, passes its judgment, recoils from the uncongenial touch, is tempted to take pleasure in their calamity, and at the same time is intensely conscious of condemnation and humiliation because of this ignominious failure in the grace of love. It sees the divine standard, "Charity suffereth long and is kind," charity maketh no account of the evil, charity is not provoked, beareth all things, believeth all things, hopeth all things, endureth all things, and yet it feels its inability to meet it. There is a painful conflict, perhaps a struggle with self, and the stronger uprising of the old spirit of prejudice and malice; and then the cry, "Oh! wretched man that I am, who shall deliver me?"

It is just at this point that Christ is revealed to us as the source of victory and the spirit of love. And, as we look away from our hearts to Him, and cling to Him in our helplessness, we find His love sufficient, and the heart is sweetly rested and filled with His thoughts, His gentleness, His divine forbearance, His forgiveness, meekness and patience, and we are strengthened according to His glorious power into all patience and longsuffering with joyfulness."

It often seems very strange to those who have just yielded themselves to God that they should be immediately thrown into circumstances more trying than they have ever experienced, and every right thing they try to do seems harder than before; but this is just God's way of impressing the lesson upon us, showing to us our own need, and throwing us upon His power and grace. When we have learned the lesson, the difficulty is always removed or made easier. It is a great thing to recognize in our trials as they meet us, not so much obstacles that have come to overwhelm us, as teachers that have met us on our way to bring us deeper lessons and higher blessings.

Another way by which the Spirit teaches us the exercise of love is by showing us God's thoughts in regard to ourselves, teaching us, like Himself, to see persons, not so much in their present character or personal unworthiness, as in their relation to Christ, and especially in the light of what His grace is working in them, and going to finally develop in their future character. God Himself looks at us, not as we are, but as we are to Christ; and loves us, not for our sake, but for Christ's sake, and for His own sake, because of something in Himself which cannot help loving even the unlovely. And then, God always looks beyond our present to the future ideal, which His love has for us, and to which, it is bringing us. God sees us, not as we are today, but as we shall be by-and-by, when He has accomplished the purpose of His grace in us, and we shall shine forth as the sun in the kingdom of our Father. And if we would, like Him, thus look at others, not of ourselves, but in Christ, and not in the present, but in light of the glorious future, we should love them as He loves them, and be lifted above all that is trying into the victory of faith and love. If we truly believe in God's purpose of grace for us, we must likewise for them.

There is nothing more beautiful than this spirit in God Himself, which refuses to recognize the faults of His children. He said, "Surely, they are my people, children that will not lie;" He was not willing to see their faults and sins. It was the blindness of love; the blessed blindness which He would teach us also, and in which we shall find our sweetest victories, and lose most of our burdens.

There is a parable of a man who met a traveler on the road, dragged down almost to the earth by an unequal burden which he carried on his shoulders. He had two sacks upon his back; one hanging in front, the other behind. The one that hung before contained the bad deeds of his neighbors, and it was so full that his head was bowed almost to the ground, while the odor that came up from the offensive mass almost suffocated him. The sack which he carried behind contained their good deeds, but it seemed almost empty, and was not able to balance the overwhelming weight that hung before. While the man was trying to persuade him to reverse the load, another traveler came up behind, walking lightly, with head erect and shining face. He, too, had two sacks upon his back, but they did not seem to oppress him, but rather to rest him. The one in front contained the good deeds of his neighbors, and he seemed to never tire of contemplating the present burdens, which, he said, instead of weighing him down seemed always to draw him forward on his journey. When the gentleman asked him what he carried in the other sack that hung behind, he said, "O, that is where I keep the bad actions of my friends;" "but," said the other, "I don't see any there." "Well," said the traveler, "I have made a little hole in the bottom of the bag, and when anything disagreeable occurs I just pitch it over my shoulder into the sack and it drops out at the bottom, and so I have nothing to hold me back, but everything to press me onward, and my journey is a very delightful and easy one."

The greatest blessing of love is the blessing that it brings to us. The heaviest curse of hate is the corrosion it leaves upon the heart. Every time a temptation comes to us to judge harshly of another, and take any pleasure in their calamity, and we pray for them instead, we have ourselves obtained a blessing far richer than theirs. Every time we linger on an injury, even in our thought, and harbor an ungracious spirit, we have eaten so much carrion, and have depleted our spiritual strength in proportion. Therefore, love is not only duty, but it is also life, and selfishness is self-destruction. Never was there a truer sentence spoken than this, "He that loveth his life shall lose it, but he that hateth his life shall keep it unto life eternal."

While it is true that the Holy Spirit will always give us the victory and grace of love, yet we have a more solemn part ourselves to perform; we must be willing to choose it, and this is often the very crisis of defeat. Pride and bitterness are not willing even to receive the love of God; some would rather have their revenge than their victory. They would not forgive even if they could, and the Lord lets them have their way, and their sin become its own avenger.

Often have we met even Christian hearts who have said, "I do not want to love some people; I shall not respect myself if I did; I take a real pleasure in disliking them." Sometimes have we been asked by a heart that has struggled long for this grace of love, "Why is it God does not give me love?" and we have looked into their face and asked, "Do you really want it? Do you really choose to love some persons, and would you be glad this moment to be able to treat them, with all your heart, with tenderness and sweetness?" and they have looked into their heart and honestly replied, "I believe I am not willing;" and in that moment they have felt that they did not really want this blessing, and therefore did not have it.

Are any of our readers in this state? Beloved, pause and remember with deep solemnity your earliest, simplest prayer, "Forgive us our trespasses as we forgive them that trespass against us." There are two unpardonable sins; one is the unbelief that rejects Christ, the other is the bitterness that refuses to love our brother. For He has said, who died for His enemies, "If ye forgive not, neither will your heavenly Father forgive you." It is vain to say we cannot love; He knows we cannot, but He is willing to give us the love if we are honestly willing to receive it, so that we are without excuse.

There are many lessons in the school of love into which we shall be led as we walk in the Spirit day by day. We shall find the love of God Himself shed abroad in our heart, and our own love to Him shall be kept alive and quickened as an ever-burning fire. It shall not always be emotion, but it shall ever be the purpose of obedience, which is the truest test of love, for He has said, "If ye love me keep my commandments." And we shall find it so utterly His love, rather than our own, that we need not watch it as a transient and uncertain feeling which we are always afraid of losing, but it will possess us as a divine principle, springing up when needed as a well of water whose fountains are in the very heart of Christ. It will be the love of Christ Himself to the Father living and working in our hearts.

So, also, will we find our natural affections intensified, and we shall love our friends more fervently than before, and yet more restfully, more purely, and more for His sake and glory, and less for their sakes and our own.

So, too, shall we find our Christian ties divinely quickened, and our love to the brethren, like the great tides of God's own heart. We shall understand the language of the Bible which speaks of our Christian fellowship and unity. Our hearts shall be knitted together in love, and we shall know what Paul meant when he spoke of the consolation in Christ, the fellowship of the Spirit, the bowels and mercies, the mutual love of Christ's disciples, until it shall be indeed true that the ties of spiritual relationship seem to be even more intense than any of the bonds of human affection.

Our love for souls shall also be thus divinely-imparted and sustained. Men and women will be laid upon our hearts until we shall long over them with an intensity of desire to which there is no parallel in human nature or experience, and it will be a luxury of joy to labor for them, minister with them, and suffer, for their sake. We shall be able to spend our lives in the very cesspools of iniquity, and not feel the hideous surroundings. Our mission rooms, crowded with poverty and sin, and the air fetid with foul breath, unclean attire, and moral pollution, shall seem to us like the gate of heaven. Joy will give radiance to our face, and wings to our feet, in the errands of ministering love. No task will seem trying, and no sinner unattractive, to one whose heart has been thus possessed with the Savior's heart of love.

Love will make that mother bear for her child humiliating drudgeries and excruciating agonies which no servile wages could bribe her to endure, and love for souls will give zest, freshness, and perpetual delight to all the ministry. "So I was had home to prison," wrote the quaint John Bunyan of the place that the love of God had made a paradise; and "I wrote because joy did make me write," was his explanation of the book that has charmed all generations. And such service for Christ, and such alone, will sustain us amid the toils and sacrifices, amid the fields of wretchedness and sin. This love the Holy Spirit alone can give, and this He will freely give to every consecrated heart that receives Him fully. This is just the spirit of His own ministry. For eighteen hundred years the Holy Spirit has dwelt in a hospital of moral leprosy and contagion, and nothing could have held Him in such scenes of sin and repulsion but love more strong than aught that mortals know of love. This earth has been His chosen home, and the heart of sinful men His willing abode; and He will shed abroad the same love in every heart that receives Him.

Beloved, shall we open all our being to His heavenly power, and enter into all the fullness of the love of God? This is the divine nature; this is the substance of heaven; this is the essence of all enduring holiness and happiness; and this the Holy Spirit longs to teach to every willing disciple.

So let us receive Him, and walk in Him, and so "walk in love."

Chapter 11: THE SPIRIT OF POWER

"Ye shall receive the power of the Holy Ghost coming upon you." Acts 1: 5.

The world is discovering, even in the scientific field, that power is not to be measured by mere mechanical and material forces. There was a time when the strength of an army could be estimated by the numbers and the fighting qualities of its soldiers, but today a small battery of artillery could destroy an entire phalanx of Nebuchadnezzar's, Alexander's, or Caesar's army.

The walls of Babylon would not stand a month against the mines and missiles of modern military science. The hand of a baby was mightier than the massive rocks of Hell Gate. The power of a sunbeam is stronger than the momentum of an iceberg. A single jet of gas will move the mechanism of machinery, when wisely applied, and we are approximating to some knowledge of the great fundamental force of electricity, which will perhaps ultimately be proved to be the principal form of material force in the natural universe. Of course, we know that power belongeth to God, and that the Holy Spirit, the Executive of the Trinity, is the dispenser and agent of the divine power.

Hence our departing Lord said "Ye shall receive the power of the Holy Ghost coming upon you." He is the personal power, and as we receive Him we are empowered for all His will and work.

Let us first consider the nature of true spiritual power.

1. It is not intellectual force. There is force in the human mind. Man can move his fellow-man by eloquence and persuasion, and can overcome the forces of matter by his ingenuity and skill; but this is not the power that the Holy Spirit gives us for the work of Christ. Often it is a hindrance to His effectual working, and it is not until our confidence in our own thoughts and reasonings has been renounced that He can "use the foolish things to confound them that are wise, and the weak things to confound them that are mighty, that no flesh should glory in His presence."

The power by which the orator sways his audience, producing deep emotion and enthusiasm, and is admired as the master of all hearts, is not the power of the Holy Ghost. The same effect may be produced by delightful music or splendid acting; and the tears of the sanctuary may be no holier than those of the opera or the theater. Even the most logical presentation of divine things, which delights the hearers and impresses the imagination and the understanding, may be utterly destitute of real spiritual power. Hence, some of the most splendid preachers of the Christian pulpit classics of the past two centuries preached almost without definite spiritual results in the known conversion of souls.

It is not the mere truth as truth that produces spiritual results, but it is the power of God accompanying it through the Holy Ghost.

2. It is not the power of organization or numbers.

Much of the power of Christianity today is the natural result of organized forces. Many a successful church owes its prosperity, in a great measure, to the business principles on which it is run, and its influence is made up largely of the social elements which constitute it, the numbers which attend it, or the effective machinery by which it is moved; but this may involve no spiritual power whatever.

It is not inconsistent with spiritual power; the Holy Ghost may work in the channels of order and systematic work, but all of this may exist in the most complete form and yet it be simply a religious club and ecclesiastical machinery.

A minister may build up his church just as a man builds up his business, and the ambition which accomplishes his splendid ideal may be of precisely the same kind as that which has founded and consummated the great financial enterprises of our age. There is a no more perfect organization in the world than Romanism. Its machinery is superb, but it knows nothing of spiritual power.

Hood has drawn the picture in the "Ancient Mariner" of a ship of death drifting across the ocean, and manned by lifeless forms of men; a dead man at the helm, a dead man in the rigging, a dead man on the bridge, a dead man on the deck, drifting in silence across the deep. Some one has represented a formal church as a ship of death, with all the forms of life, but without the life; a dead man in the pulpit, and dead souls in the pews, while the voice of heaven sadly complains, "Thou hast a name that thou livest, and art dead."

Some writers are very fond of quoting statistics of Christianity, and speaking of the four or five hundred million who today are under Christian governments, so called, and the more than three hundred million who are nominally Christians. If we were to deduct from these figures the numbers who belong to the Papal church, and then the members of national Protestant establishments, which do not even profess to admit members on the ground of conversion, there would be a frightful deduction, and a very small remnant who might even be claimed as genuine Christians. How many would be left who even would themselves admit that they knew nothing of the power of the Holy Spirit? Spiritual power may operate without any organized basis. Like the torrent, it is very apt to break through the banks and barriers and sweep over the church of God regardless of its forms and formalities.

In our own day God has been pleased to give it in the most eminent degree, to the men and women that are not even members of the formal circle of the ordained ministry, but have been chosen by God partly because they represented none of the elements which are usually connected with power. We can have this power under any circumstances, and the feeblest church, the most isolated worker, the least influential minister of Christ, may become an instrument of blessing to the whole church of God.

I. What is Spiritual Power?

1. It is the power which convicts of sin. It is the power that makes the hearers to see themselves as God sees them, and humbles them in the dust. It sends people home from the house of God not feeling better but worse; not always admiring the preacher, but often so tried that they perhaps resolve that they will never hear him again. But they know from their inmost soul that he is right and they are wrong. It is the power of conviction; the power that awakens the conscience and says to the soul, "Thou art the man;" it is the power of which the apostle speaks in connection with his own ministry, "by manifestation of the truth, commending ourselves to every

man's conscience in the sight of God."

They that possess this power will not always be popular preachers, but they will always be effectual workers. Sometimes the hearer will almost think that they are personal, and that someone has disclosed to them his secret sins. Speaking of such a sermon, one of our most honored evangelists said that he felt so indignant with the preacher under whom he was converted that he waited for some time near the door for the purpose of giving him a trashing for daring to expose him in the way he had done, thinking that somebody had informed on him.

Let us covet this power. It is the very stamp and seal of the Holy Ghost on a faithful minister.

After some of Mr. Moody's evangelistic meetings, it is said that thousands and thousands of dollars have been returned anonymously, or otherwise, to the original owners. Men's consciences have been awakened; the power of God has arraigned them before the bar of justice.

2. It is the power that lifts up Christ and makes Him real to the apprehension of the hearer.

Some sermons leave upon the mind a vivid impression of the truth; others leave upon the mind the picture of the Savior. It is not so much an idea as a person. This is true preaching, and this is the Holy Spirit's most blessed and congenial ministry. He loves to draw in heavenly lines the face of Jesus, and make Him shine out over every page of the Bible, and every paragraph of the sermon as a face of beauty and a heart of love.

Let us cultivate this power, for this is what the struggling, hungry world wants, to know its Savior. "We would see Jesus" is still its cry; and the answer still is, "I, if I be lifted up from the earth, will draw all men unto me."

3. This power leads men to decision. It is not merely that they know something they did not know before, that they get new thoughts and conceptions of truth which they carry away to remember and reflect upon, nor even that they feel the deepest and most stirring emotions of religious feeling, but the power of the Spirit always presses them to action, prompt, decisive, positive action.

This is the best test of power. It was the test of ancient eloquence; it was the glory of Demosthenes that while under the eloquence of other orators the multitudes hurrahed for the speaker; under his matchless tongue they forgot all about Demosthenes and shouted with one voice, "Let us go and fight Philip."

The power of the Holy Ghost leads men to decide for God, and to enlist against Satan, to give up habits of sin, and to make great and everlasting decisions.

The Lord grant us so to speak in His name, in demonstration of the Spirit and power, that the result shall be, as Paul himself expresses it on writing to the Thessalonians, "Our word came unto you not in word only, but in power, and ye turned from idols to serve the living and true God, and to wait for His Son from heaven, even Jesus, which saved us from the wrath to come."

II. The Elements and Sources of Power.

1. It is the power of Christ. It is His own personal working both in the worker and upon the hearers. "All power," He says, "is given unto me in heaven and on earth, and lo! I am with you always even unto the end of the age."

Power is not given unto us, but unto Him, and we are constantly to recognize His living and perpetual presence, and to count upon His direct working. If, therefore, we would have this power, we must be personally united to Him and have Him as an abiding presence. God does not want to glorify us and to show to the world our importance, but to glorify His Son Jesus Christ, and hold up His power and glory.

2. It is the power of the Holy Spirit.

He is the agent who reveals Christ, and manifests His mighty working; therefore, the power is directly connected with the Spirit personally, in the very promise of Christ respecting the Comforter. "When He is come He shall convict the world of sin, and of righteousness, and of judgment." It is not said that we shall convict, but that He shall convict, operating both in the worker and in the hearer's hearts.

So, again, in the promise of Christ just before His ascension, it is said, "Ye shall receive the power of the Holy Ghost coming upon you;" it is not power through the Holy Ghost, but it is the very power of the personal Holy Spirit.

In the account of 1 Cor. 12, of the gifts of the Spirit that were to remain in the New Testament church, all are directly connected with the personal working of the Holy Ghost, "To one is given faith, by the Spirit; to another the working of miracles;" but, lest in any case the power should be connected with the individual in any undue personal sense, it is added, "All these worketh that one and the self-same Spirit, dividing to every man severally as he will."

The history of the Christian church has no more striking feature or lesson than that connected with the phenomena of the Spirit of power. All that have been mightily used of God in the conversion of souls, and the building up of the kingdom of Christ, have recognized His personal baptism as the secret of their power. It was after He had come upon Peter at Pentecost that three thousand souls were converted by a very simple message. It was His fiery truth that made George Whitfield the power of God unto the salvation of innumerable thousands. It was He who fell upon Charles Finney and his audiences, and so filled the whole town, sometimes, where he ministered, with the Divine Presence, that the hands in the factories would fall down at their work and begin to plead for mercy. It is to the day when He fell upon an illiterate Sunday-school worker on the public streets, until he wept for holy joy, that Dwight Moody traces back all his unparalleled usefulness. And many a lowlier worker could tell of a similar story of weakness changed to might, and ignorance made into a channel of divine teaching and blessing through the power of the Holy Ghost in a consecrated heart and life.

Let us honor Him as the personal source of all spiritual power, and He will surely honor us. He holds the key to every human heart, He is the source of the highest thought and the truest feeling, and He has given to us our equipment for our holy ministry for Christ, and we may boldly claim His all-sufficient power and presence.

3. The power of truth.

When united to Christ and accompanied by the Holy Spirit, the gospel is the power of God unto salvation. Apart from the Spirit it is only "the letter that killeth," but accompanied by the Holy Ghost it is wonderfully and divinely adapted to convict of sin, to lead to Christ, and to establish the foundations of faith, hope, love, and holy character. It is not the way we present the gospel, but it is the pure and simple gospel itself which is the power of God, the fundamental elements of the gospel, especially the glorious truth that Christ has died for our sins, and brought in an everlasting righteousness and salvation by His resurrection and intercession.

It is simply wonderful how God uses the plain statement of the gospel oftentimes for the salvation of souls. The sermons of Peter and Paul in the Acts of the Apostles are destitute of either logic or rhetoric. They are simply statements of the great fact that Christ has died and risen to save men, and that by simply accepting this message we are saved. It does indeed seem foolish in its weakness, and yet again and again has God shown that it has the power to change the human heart as nothing else has. How stupendous its result at Pentecost when thousands were saved under the simple proclamation! How marvelous its fruits wherever Paul proclaimed it, not with wisdom of words, but purposely in great simplicity, lest it should be made of none effect!

The early missionaries in Greenland supposed that they must spend a long time in preliminary teaching, preparing the natives to understand the gospel; and so they taught them the principles of the Old Testament, the law of God, etc., but without spiritual fruit; but one day, when the missionary happened to read the story of the third of John, the old chief was overwhelmed with wonder and joy, and immediately spiritual fruit began, and he and many of his people gladly accepted the Savior of sinners.

One of the most remarkable results that we ever saw follow a single sermon, occurred through the preaching of a plain evangelist, especially on one occasion when his discourse was, humanly speaking, weaker than ever before, lacking animation and rhetorical effect, and consisting simply of a clear, plain, and rather a dry statement of the resurrection of Jesus Christ, as the ground of the sinner's hope. But the Holy Spirit used that simple truth to the conversion of a great number of people that night, many of whom remain until this day monuments of the grace of God.

There is in the gospel itself a divine potency that we may fully trust, when we present it in the power of the Spirit, to become God's instrument unto the salvation of all that believe. It has power to transform the whole eternal destiny of the soul, and to change its entire views of God and motives of life.

Let us be sure that we do not dilute its power by trying to mix with it our human reasonings, and let us be careful that we do not depend unduly upon the clearness or persuasiveness of our appeal but wholly upon the truth of the gospel itself, and the power of the Spirit that accompanies it.

4. The personal qualities which the Spirit produces in the instruments through whom He works. For, while the Spirit is the worker, He prepares the vessel through whom He works to be a fitting instrument for His service.

Let us look at some of the elements of power with which the Holy Spirit endues the consecrated heart.

1. Perhaps the most obvious quality in such a person would be earnestness; that intense fusing of

all the capacities of the soul and being into one's work.

It is the secret of success even in human affairs, but it is preeminently the very element of power in Christian workers. It is a quality which the hearer instinctively discovers, and whose absence is fatal to effectiveness, notwithstanding all other gifts. Its essential root is sincerity and honesty of purpose. It was this which made the Master say, "My meat is to do the will of Him that sent me, and to finish His work." It was this which enabled Paul to exclaim, "If we be beside ourselves it is to God; for the love of Christ constraineth us." "My heart's desire and prayer to God for Israel is that they might be saved."

This was the secret of Whitfield's wonderful power; his whole soul was engrossed in his work. His one business was to preach the gospel and win souls. No sacrifice could appease him or deter him from his delightful task. It was an enthusiasm with him, and so it is with every earnest soul. This is the true meaning of the word enthusiasm, which literally signifies, God within us. Where the Holy Spirit possesses the heart there always is intense enthusiasm. The true minister should be both a burning and shining light, and the baptism of fire is always a baptism of intense earnestness.

2. Another element of spiritual power is holiness.

There is a certain atmosphere which a saintly soul carries with him which communicates itself to others, and is instinctively perceived even by the careless. There are men and women who awaken in all they come in contact with an irresistible respect, and even reverence. The spirit of godliness, like the nature of the rose, betrays itself in the look, the tone, the bearing, and awakens an unconscious response even in the hearts of ungodly men. The good man compels the homage of the bad, even when they hate and persecute him. The very look of the saintly MeCheyne often filled the hearts of his hearers with strange solemnity. The tones with which George Whitfield pronounced the simplest word sometimes made people weep. The godless Chesterfield declared, after a visit to Fenelon, that another day in his house would have made him a Christian in spite of himself. The very factory hands were sometimes smitten with conviction at their work as Charles Finney passed through the room. The influence of the Countess of Huntington was such, through her simple piety, that even her profligate king respected her, and said that He would be glad to go to heaven clinging to her skirts.

It is possible for us, like a spice-ship entering the harbor and filling the air with fragrance, so to bear about with us the atmosphere of heaven that it shall be true of us as it was of the apostles, "We are a sweet savor of Christ unto them that believe, and unto them that perish. To the one we are the savor of life unto life, and to the other of death unto death; and who is sufficient for these things?"

The Christian worker and divine messenger who comes to men fresh from communion with the skies, will have, like Moses, "some of the glory upon his brow, and the world will again take knowledge of him that he has been with Jesus." It was said of the good Mr. Aitkin, of England, the father of the well-known evangelist, that one always felt in his presence as though encompassed with the very presence of God. He seemed to carry Christ so about with him that people forgot the man in the overshadowing glory of the Master. This is the honor and the power which He will bestow upon every consecrated servant.

Let it be our high ambition thus to carry the seal of God upon our brow, and the witness of heaven in our every attitude, and look, and tone.

3. Faith is another element of spiritual power imparted by the Holy Ghost.

Our success will bear proportion to our expectation of results. The motto of the effective worker will be, "We believe, and therefore have we spoken."

A minister complained to Mr. Spurgeon that he thought that he must give up his ministry, and doubted if he had ever been called to it, giving as a reason that he had labored untiringly for four years, and had not seen a single fruit from his ministry. Mr. Spurgeon simply asked: "Have you always preached expecting conversions at each service?" He acknowledged that he had never thought of such a thing, but had eagerly desired them, and wondered that they did not come, "Why," said the good minister, "you did not expect them, and you did not receive them; God's condition of blessing is faith; and it is as necessary for our work as for our salvation."

This is, indeed, true; it is not in proportion to our desperate efforts that we should see the results; but to our simple trust in the power of God, to honor His own Word, and work by His own Spirit in the hearts of men. The most of the great revival movements have thus begun.

A humble working man in the north of Ireland read the story of George Muller's life, and immediately thought, why cannot I have the same answer to prayer in the salvation of souls? He immediately began to pray for a great outpouring of the Holy Spirit upon his city and country; soon he was joined by another, and then another, and before long a flood of fire was sweeping over all the land, and hundreds of thousands of souls were mightily converted to God. It was thus that Mr. Finney always prepared for his work. We can read in his biography how he used to retire with a friend, sometimes into the woods, and spend hours on his knees until he felt the blessing was claimed and the power was coming, and then he would go forth about his work with the tranquil certainty that God was there and would be revealed in all His power and glory, and the result always was the mighty working of the Holy Ghost.

Not always is it the preacher who exercises the effectual faith; sometimes it is a silent and obscure heart whom no one shall know until the day when all things shall be revealed.

A celebrated preacher of the middle ages was always accompanied by a quiet and insignificant man, without whom he would never preach. The man never opened his lips in public, and seemed to be a useless appendage. He afterwards explained that while he preached his companion prayed, and that he attributed all the marvelous results of his messages to his believing intercessions. There is no Christian but can thus claim and exercise the very power of God even in the most silent capacity, and it will be found in the great day that God has not failed to credit the recompense to the real instrument through whom the divine working came. It will very likely be found in that day that the voice that spake from the pulpit had but a fractional share in the real work which the Holy Ghost accomplished, but that some humble saint was the real channel through whom the fire of God fell upon, convicted and converted souls.

But it is not only for the conversion of souls that God will give us His power, and faith to claim His working, but for everything connected with His cause, and our ministry shall touch every part of His work.

Faith is the true channel of effectiveness, simply because faith is merely the hand by which the forces of Omnipotence are brought to bear upon the work. The removing of obstacles, the influencing of human hearts and minds, the bringing together of workers, the obtaining of helpers, the supply of financial needs; all these are proper subjects for believing prayer, and proper lines for demonstrating the all-sufficiency of God. And if, instead of begging for help, and compromising the honor of Christ by despairing appeals to the church and the world, the people of God would more simply trust Him, they would be saved a thousand embarrassments, and His name would be constantly glorified in the manifestation of His all-sufficiency before an unbelieving world.

A few stupendous examples of God's faithfulness in answering the prayers of His people in the supply of money and men, such as have been afforded by the story of George Muller's Orphanage, the China Inland Mission, and similar works by faith, were not intended to be isolated instances, but to prove to the world that Christ is able always to meet His people's needs, and to be but samples of a principle which should be the rule of Christian work; that God in all things might be glorified through Jesus Christ, not only in the spiritual, but in the temporal and practical needs of His kingdom.

4. Love.

Still more necessary is the spirit of love as the very element and character of every true Christian worker. "Lovest thou me?" is the prime condition on which Christ's saints are to minister to His flock, and love for souls is the only bond that can win and hold them and can sustain our own heart amid the trials and discouragements of Christian work. Human love will make any task a delight. For the child of her affection the mother can toil and suffer without weariness, and count life itself a small sacrifice for her loved one.

And so the love of souls will inspire us and sustain us in the face of every discouragement and disagreeable surrounding, until the most loathsome and offensive scenes will be a delight to us, and the most coarse and degraded souls will be dear to our hearts as our beloved friends, and it shall become the passion of our life to win them for Christ.

A noble woman died lately in Indiana, who had a remarkable record of success in dealing with hardened women. She was the superintendent of a large institution for this class, and her influence over them was irresistible; it was the power of love. Often when met by stormy passion and wild, coarse, desperate wickedness, has she thrown her arms about some degraded woman, and by a kiss of unfeigned love and the hot tears of her tender compassion, melted the heart of stone. We must love people if we would do them good, but such love must be divine. Mere human sympathy does not go to the depths of their heart, but the love which is born of God and inbreathed of the Holy Ghost, always finds its way to every citadel of rebellion, and wins the soul for God.

At a railway station a brutal criminal was being conveyed to the penitentiary. Sitting on the benches with his keepers, he was awaiting the incoming train. A little girl sat watching him beside her father. Her heart was overwhelmed with the strange sight, and at length she stole up to him, unnoticed by her father, and looking earnestly in his face, she said, while the tears were in her eyes, "Poor man, I am so sorry for you" The shock aroused him for a moment to realize his condition; his eye flashed, his frame shook with passion, and he repelled her from his presence as though he had been insulted, and almost tried to strike her. She cowered back to her father's knee, the tears still in her eyes, and still watched him; but in a little while she managed to slip away again from the arms of her father, who supposed she had been frightened effectually away from approaching him, and stealing up to him again she looked once more in his hideous face and said very slowly, "Poor man, Jesus Christ is so sorry for you." Instantly he seemed utterly changed and subdued. That name had power to overcome the demon in his heart; his wild defiance broke quite down and he began to weep like a child. Years after he often told the story himself, when a happy, useful Christian man, and he said it was that message that broke his heart, and never left him till he found the Savior. It was not the child's love merely, but the Savior's love in the child that won.

There is much danger of turning the gospel of Christ and the power of God into human sentiment. Mere compassion for people, and even a costly show of interest and sympathy, will not save them, but the love born of the Holy Ghost will go as deep as the height from which it springs; and if we walk in the Spirit we shall find Him ever breathing upon us in our work that love which will brood over souls with a divine motherhood, loving them even before we know them, praying for them in the Spirit before we have singled them out of our audience; and then when we meet them recognizing them with a thrill of joy as the souls that we have been bearing on our hearts as a burden of prayer.

This love will strangely endear to us the most repulsive beings and make the most dreadful scenes more delightful than the surroundings of culture and affection, and a life of luxury and indulgence. This is the passion that has drawn so many noble men and women to the wretched fields of sin, until their heavenly love has gathered, like the magnet to itself, the lost and wretched, and bound them forever to the heart of Christ. This is the sweetest, highest gift of the Holy Ghost; the most tender, irresistible element of spiritual power. This was the force that drew souls to Jesus.

Chapter 12: THE SPIRIT OF PRAYER

"Likewise the Spirit also helpeth our infirmities; for we know not what we should pray for as we ought; but the Spirit itself maketh intercession for us with groanings which cannot be uttered." Rom. 8: 26.

"Praying in the Holy Ghost." Jude, verse 20.

The mystery of prayer! There is nothing like it in the natural universe. A higher and a lower being in perfect communion. A familiar intercourse, yet both as widely distinct as the finite is from the infinite. More wonderful even than that we should be able to hold converse with the insect that crawls beneath our feet, or the bird that flutters on the branches at our window! Marvelous bond of prayer which can span the gulf between the Creator and the creature, the infinite God and the humblest and most illiterate child!

How has this been accomplished? The three Divine persons have all cooperated in opening the gates of prayer. The Father waits at the throne of grace as the hearer of prayer; the Son has come to reveal the Father, and has returned to be our Advocate in His presence. And the Holy Spirit *with reason*

has come still nearer, as the other Advocate in the heart, to teach us the heavenly secret of prayer, and send up our petitions in the true spirit to the hands of our heavenly Intercessor. It is to this ministry we are to speak now.

The very name given to the Holy Ghost, literally means the Advocate, and the chief business of the one Advocate is to prepare our cause in the office, and the other to plead it before the Judge. We have the whole Trinity in our behalf. The Holy Spirit prepares our case, the Lord Jesus presents it, and the Judge is our Father. What an infinite light, and what an unspeakable comfort this sheds on the subject of prayer!

Our need of this Advocate is referred to in our text very impressively: "We know not what to pray for as we ought." We are often ignorant of the subjects for which we ought to pray; and often, when we know our needs, we know not how rightly to present them. There is much expressed in these words. We are often deeply ignorant of our truest needs, and the things we wish most for are not the things we most require. Our minds are blinded by prejudice and passion; the things we would sometimes ask for we shall afterwards find would have been only an injury. Besides, we know not the future, and cannot, intelligently, anticipate the needs and dangers against which we should pray, while a thousand unseen elements of peril continually surround us and need a wiser forethought and insight than our own to guard against.

And often "we know not how to pray as we ought." Prayer is a high art, and must be divinely taught. We would not rashly send a crude and unprepared case before an earthly tribunal, and he is greatly mistaken who thinks that the thoughtless and random dashes of human impulse, or even sincere earthly desires, are all accepted as prayer. Many "receive not because they ask amiss." If we regard iniquity in our hearts the Lord will not hear us. We must ask in faith, nothing doubting. These and other qualities must be taught and impelled by the Holy Spirit. "We know not how to pray as we ought."

The right motive which seeks supremely the glory of God, the right spirit recognizing submissively and joyfully His sovereign will, the deep and sincere desire, the faith which dares to ask as largely as the measure of the Father's will and promise, the patience that tarries if it waits, knowing that it will surely come, and will not tarry too long, the obedience that steps out upon the promise all these elements of prayer are operations of the Holy Spirit, and we cannot too devoutly thank Him that He is willing thus to teach our ignorance and simplicity the heavenly secret of prayer. "The Spirit helpeth our infirmities, and maketh intercession within us, with groanings which cannot be uttered."

1. The Holy Spirit reveals to us our needs. This is always the first element in prayer, a painful consciousness of failure and necessity. The prophet's word to Jehoshaphat was, "Make the valley full of ditches," and then, the second, "The valley shall be full of water." The heart must be ploughed up into great channels of conscious need to hold the blessing when it comes; and this is often painful work, but, "Blessed are they which hunger and thirst after righteousness, for they shall be filled."

When the Spirit of grace and supplication is poured out upon Jerusalem, the effect is a deep and universal sorrow. "They shall look upon Him they have pierced, and they shall mourn as one that mourneth for an only son, and be in bitterness as one is in bitterness for a firstborn." The Spirit of prayer is the spirit of dependence, deep humility and conscious need.

2. The Holy Spirit next awakens in the soul holy desires for the blessings that God is about to give. Desire is an element in prayer. "Whatever things ye desire," our Lord says, "when ye pray believe that ye receive them." These deep, spiritual longings are like the rootlets by which the plant draws the nourishment from the soil; like the absorbing vessels of the human system, which take in and assimilate nourishment and food. The desires give intensity and force to our prayer, and enlarge the heart to receive the blessing when it comes. God, therefore, often keeps His children waiting for the visible answer to their petitions, in order that they may the more ardently desire the blessing, and be thus enabled to receive it more fully and appreciate it more gratefully when it comes.

When we were traveling in Italy we were often serenaded by parties of native musicians, whose sweet strains were sometimes very delightful. But we noticed that whenever we paid them their little gratuity they always stopped the music and they went away, and when we wished to listen longer to their sweetest strains, we waited before handing them their charity. So God loves to hear His people's holy desires and earnest prayers, and often prolongs the petition because He delights to hear us pray, and then gives us the larger blessing in proportion to our waiting. Often has your heart longed for some special blessing until it seemed that it would break for desire. You almost thought that you never should possess the holiness you so longed for. But now, as you look back, you see that this deep hunger was just the beginning of your blessing. It was the shadow side, the Holy Ghost awakening all the receptive capacities of your being, to absorb it when it came.

Once we saw a party of children sending up a balloon of tissue paper. First, the balloon was carefully constructed of the lightest fabric, and then suspended with light cords a few feet above the ground. Its little beacon light was attached, and then they began to prepare the force that was to be used for its ascension. It was nothing more than simply building a little fire below the open mouth of the balloon and allowing the heated air to ascend until it filled the entire space within. The moment this was done the little vessel swelled and reached out for its ascension, pulling hard at the restraining cords, and pressing upwards. When it was thoroughly filled with the heated air it was only necessary to cut the cords, and instantly it sailed away to the upper air. So it seems the warm breath of holy desire and earnest purpose in prayer, when inspired by the Holy Ghost, bears up our petitions to the throne of grace, and makes the difference between the mere words of formalism, and the "effectual working prayer of the righteous man which availeth much."

3. The Holy Spirit lays upon the heart wherein He dwells the special burden of prayer. We often read in the old prophetic Scriptures of the burden of the Lord. And so still the Lord lays His burden on His consecrated messengers. This is the meaning of the strong language of our text, "The Spirit maketh intercession within us with groanings which cannot be uttered." Sometimes this burden is inarticulate and unintelligible even to the supplicant himself. Perhaps some heavy shadow rests upon the soul, some deep depression, some crushing weight under which we can only groan. With it there may come the definite thought of some personal need, some apprehended evil that overhangs us, or some dear one who is brought to our spirit as somehow connected with this pressure. As we pray for this especial person or thing, light seems to open upon the heart, and an assurance of having met the will of God in our prayer; or sometimes the

burden is not understood; and yet, as it presses heavily upon us and we hold it up to Him who does understand, we are conscious that our prayer is not in vain; but that He who knows its meaning and prompts its cry, is granting what He sees to be best under the circumstances for us or others, as the burden may apply.

We may never know in this world just what it meant, and yet, often we will find that some great trial has been averted, some impending danger turned aside, some difficulty overcome, some sufferer relieved, some soul saved.

It is not necessary that we should always know; indeed, perhaps we should never fully know what any of our prayers wholly mean; God's answer is always larger than our petition, and even when our prayer is most definite and intelligent there is a wide margin which only the Holy Ghost can interpret, and God will fill it up in His infinite wisdom and love. That is what is meant by the significant language of the text, "He that searcheth the heart knoweth what is the mind of the Spirit, for He maketh intercession for the saints according to the will of God." The Father is always searching our hearts and listening, not to our wild and often mistaken outcries, but to the mind of the Holy Spirit in us, whom He recognizes as our true guardian and monitor, and He grants us according to His petitions and not merely our words. But if we walk in the Spirit and are trained to know and obey His voice, we shall not send up the wild and vain outcries of our mistaken impulses, but shall echo His will and His prayer, and thus shall ever pray in accordance with the will of God.

The sensitive spirit grows very quick to discern God's voice. That which would naturally be considered as simple depression of spirits comes to be instantly recognized as a hint that God has something to say to us, or something to ask in us for ourselves or others. Often our physical sensations come to be quick, instinctive interpreters of some inward call; for when we do not quickly listen to God's voice He knocks more loudly, until the very body feels the pain and warns us that the Lord hath need of us. If we were but more watchful we would find that nothing comes to us at any moment of our lives which has not some divine significance, and which does not lead us in some way to communion or service. He who thus walks with God soon learns the luxury of having no personal burdens or troubles, but recognizing everything as service for God or for others.

This makes the ministry of prayer a very solemn responsibility, for, if we are not obedient to His voice, some interest must suffer, some part of His will be neglected, some part of His purpose frustrated, so far, at least, as our cooperation is concerned, and, perhaps, someone very dear to us will lose a blessing through our neglect or disobedience; or we ourselves find that we are not prepared for the conflict or trial against which He was providing by the very burden that we would not understand nor carry.

Thus it was with the disciples and the Master in the garden of Gethsemane. That was for Him the anticipation of the cross; and, as He met the burden in advance, He was prepared for the awful hours that followed, and went through them in victory, and thus redeemed the world. But the disciples could not watch with Him one hour; they neglected the call to prayer, and slept when they should have hearkened and prayed, and the result was that the morning found them unprepared, and the trial ended in shameful failure, and only His previous intercession for him saved Peter from entire wreck, and perhaps a fate desperate as that of Judas.

God has placed within our breast a monitor who is always looking forward to our needs and anticipating our situations; let us, therefore, be quick to hearken and obey His voice, as He calls us to the ministry of prayer, and in so doing we shall not only save ourselves, but also many a heart that perhaps is not able to pray for itself.

tritheism

4. The Spirit brings to our hearts, in the ministry of prayer, the encouragement of God's Word, the promises of His grace, and the fulness of Christ to meet our need. It is He who gives us such conceptions of Christ as awaken in us confidence of blessing. He opens to our vision the infinite resources of the grace of God, and shows us all the rich provision of our Father's house. He unfolds to us the grounds of faith in the gospel, and teaches us to understand our redemption rights, our filial claims, and our high calling in Christ Jesus. He breathes in our heart the Spirit of sonship, and He inspires the faith which is the essential condition of effectual prayer. And so He leads us to present to the Father, in the name of the Lord Jesus, not only the right desires, but in the right spirit: "By one Spirit we have access unto the Father."

Thus He is in us the Spirit of faith, the Spirit of adoption, the Spirit of liberty in prayer, the Spirit of holy confidence and enlargement of heart, and the witnessing Spirit, who, when we pray in faith, seals upon our soul the divine assurance that our prayer is accepted before God, and that the answer will be surely given. We must first, however, believe God's promise in the exercise of simple faith, and, as we do, the Spirit witnesseth with our spirit and often fills the soul with joy and praise which anticipates the answer long before it is apparent. This is the highest triumph of prayer, to look within the veil, even before the curtains are parted, and know that our petition is granted; to hear the sound of the bells upon our High Priest's garment, even from the inmost chambers, and to rejoice in the anticipation of our blessing as fully as if we already saw its complete fulfillment.

Our Lord always requires this faith as the condition of answered prayer. "Whatsoever things ye desire, when ye pray, believe that ye receive them, and ye shall have them." "Let him ask in faith, nothing doubting. For he that wavereth is like a wave of the sea, driven with the wind and tossed. Let not that man think that he shall receive anything of the Lord." But this is the special work of the Holy Ghost. He is the Spirit of revelation and of faith, and as we pray in His fellowship, and according to His will, we shall be enabled through His grace to ask with humble and confident expectation of His blessing.

5. The Holy Spirit will also teach us when to cease from prayer, and turn our petition into thanksgiving, or go out in obedience to meet the answer as it waits before us, or comes to meet us. There is a place for silence as well as prayer, and when we truly believe, we shall cease to ask as we asked before, and henceforth our prayers shall simply be in the attitude of waiting for our answer, or holding up God's promise to him in the Spirit of praise and expectation.

This does not mean that we shall never think any more about that for which we asked, but we shall think no more of it in a doubtful manner; we shall think of it only with thanksgiving and restful expectation. We may often remind God of it, but it will always be in the spirit of trust and confidence. Therefore, the prophet speaks of those who are "the Lord's remembrancers," those that remind God of His promises and wait upon Him for His fulfillment of them. This is really a spirit of prayer, and yet it is not perhaps a spirit of petition so much as praise, which indeed is the true exhibition of the highest form of faith.

Sometimes, too, after our prayer, the Holy Spirit will have a subsequent ministry of obedience for us; there will be something for us perhaps to do in receiving the answer, and He will show us, interpreting to us God's providences as they meet us, and enabling us to meet them in a spirit of cooperation and vigilance.

He also will be present to support our faith in its tests and painful trials, and enable us to rejoice and praise God, often amid the seeming contradictions of His Providence. For faith is always tested, and "we have need of patience, that having done the will of God we might receive the promise."

Chapter 13: COOPERATING WITH THE HOLY GHOST

"Receive ye the Holy Ghost." John 20: 22.

"Be filled with the Spirit." Eph. 5: 18.

While we recognize the sovereign power of the Holy Ghost, visiting the heart at His pleasure, and working according to His will upon the objects of His grace, yet God has ordained certain laws of operation and cooperation in connection with the application of redemption; and He Himself most delicately recognizes His own laws, and respects the freedom of the human will; not forcing His blessings upon unwilling hearts, but knocking at the door of our heart, waiting to be recognized and claimed, and then working in the soul as we heartily cooperate, hearken, and obey. There is, therefore, a very solemn and responsible part for every man in cooperating with, or resisting and hindering the Holy Spirit.

"The manifestation of the Spirit is given to every man to profit withal," that is to say, it rests with the man who receives the first movement of the Holy Spirit to determine how far he will embrace his opportunity, cooperate with his heavenly Friend, and enter into all the fullness of the good and perfect will of God.

Perhaps the pound, represented in the parable as given to every one of the servants, was meant to express that gift of the Spirit which every Christian receives, and the various uses which the servants made of this common enduement may represent the degrees with which the children of God double and use their spiritual advantages.

One improved his pound until it had become ten; another until it had increased five-fold, and another neglected it and hid it in the earth. So, three men receiving in the beginning of their experience an equal measure of spiritual things, may show in the end just as great a diversity in the use that they have made of the precious trust. By a diligent and vigilant obedience the one has grown to be a Paul, crowned with ransomed souls, and clothed with all the fullness of heavenly power. The other has become, perhaps, a proud Diotrephes, seeking chiefly his personal ambition and using the divine grace for his own advantage.

The Holy Spirit is especially sensitive to the reception He finds in the human heart; never intruding as an unwelcome guest, but gladly entering every open door, and following up every invitation with His faithful love and power. How are we to cooperate with Him, and how may we grieve and hinder Him?

1. We are commanded to receive the Holy Ghost.

This denotes an active and positive taking of His life and power into our hearts and lives. It is not a mere acquiescence in His coming, or passive assent unto His will, but an active appropriating and absorbing of His blessed person and influences into our whole person. It is one thing to have our dinner brought to us, and it is another thing to eat it, drink it, assimilate it, and be nourished by it.

It is thus that we are to receive the Holy Ghost, with an open, yielding, hungering, thirsting, believing, accepting and absorbing heart, even as the dry sand receives the rain, as the empty sponge receives the moisture, as the negative cloud receives the current from the positive, as the vacuum receives the air, and the babe drinks in the mother's life from her offered breast.

There are spiritual organs of reception as well as physical. There are vessels of heart-hunger and absorption which can be cultivated and exercised, and there are those who, "by reason of use," have their senses thus exercised to receive the grace of God.

Are we receiving the Holy Ghost? are we taking the water of life freely? are we putting forth our hand grasping the tree of life and eating of its fruit?

Let us remember that we are receiving a person, and that in order to do so we must recognize that person individually, and treat Him as we would a welcome guest.

Have we thus received the Holy Spirit as a person, invited Him into our hearts, believed that He really came, and then begun to treat Him as an actual person; to talk to Him, to commune with Him, to enjoy His fellowship, to call upon His help, and practically recognize Him as a present Guest.

Not only do we receive the Holy Spirit as a person, but having thus recognized Him we are to receive His influences as He imparts them, to be open to His touch, attentive to His voice, responsive to His love, and empty vessels for His constant use and filling.

2. We are to be filled with the Spirit.

While it is true that there is a definite moment when the Holy Spirit comes to reside in the heart, yet there are repeated experiences of His renewing, quickening, reviving, refreshing influences; these are called by the apostle, in Jude, "the renewings of the Holy Ghost," which He sheds on us abundantly, and by Peter, in the Acts of the Apostles, "the times of refreshing from the presence of the Lord." The expression, "baptized of the Spirit" may be applied perhaps to our first marked experience of this kind, and in this connection we are glad that the term 'baptism' means a very thorough and complete immersion in the ocean of His love and fullness. But it is not once that He is asked to manifest His love and power.

We read in the Acts of the Apostles that after the day of Pentecost there came another day when the disciples were assembled in a time of peril and trial in prayer before the Master for His interposition, and that when they had prayed, the place was shaken where they had assembled, and they were all filled with the Holy Ghost, and the mighty power of God was manifested afresh in their midst.

And so the Apostle says in Ephesians, "Be not drunk with wine, but be filled with the Spirit." The filling of the Spirit is here contrasted with the exciting influence of earthly stimulants, as if he had said, there is one draught of which you can never drink too much; you can safely be intoxicated with the Holy Ghost.

In the twelfth chapter of First Corinthians, Paul uses the same expression in connection with the figure of baptism: "By one Spirit have we all been baptized into one body, and been made to drink of that one Spirit." It is the figure of being submerged in the ocean, and then, when lost in the depths of the sea, opening our mouths and beginning to drink of its depth and fullness. We are plunged in the Holy Spirit until He becomes the element of our being, like the air in which we move, and then we open all the faculties of our being and drink from His inexhaustible supplies.

How great the capacity of the human soul to be filled with the life of God it is impossible to say. Surely, if the sun can fill a flower with its glorious light in all the many-tinted colors; surely, if the cloud can drink in his rays until they grow with all the tints of light, O, surely the human soul can absorb all there is in God and then give it forth in the reflected light of holiness. Surely, if the earth can drink in the rain, and then give it out in the plants, and fruits, and flowers of summer, the human heart can draw from God the elements of His very being, and turn them into all the fruits of holy living and useful deeds. Surely, if His own beloved Son could dwell in His bosom ages upon ages before an angel ever sang or a planet swept along its heavenly way, or an object of creation filled the plains of immensity, and found in His Father's heart the rapture of His joy, so that He could say, "I was daily His delight, rejoicing always before Him," O, surely, the human soul can fill all its little vessels and satisfy the measure of its capacities in His divine love and benignity.

Let us receive Him in all His fullness, let us be filled with the Spirit, let us drink of the ocean in which we have been baptized. A Christian friend wrote the other day that his old neighbors had got up a report that he had turned out badly in his Christian life and taken to drinking. He replied, very happily, that it was true he had taken to drinking of late, but that if his old friends could only know what he was drinking then they would all join him, for he had found the fountain of living waters, and was drinking from the Holy Spirit and could say, "He that drinketh of this water shall never thirst again."

3. Let us trust the Holy Spirit.

We must believe in the Spirit as well as in the Son, and treat Him with confidence, expecting Him to meet us and bless us, and communicate unto Him all our needs, perplexities, and even our temptations and sins. He was the antitype of the water of Horeb's ancient rock, and it is as wrong today as it was for Moses to strike that rock in unbelieving violence, when God bids us simply to speak to it in gentleness and trust, and expect its waters to gush forth at our whispered call and satisfy out every need.

The Holy Spirit is sensitive to our distrust. Many persons cry for Him and pray to Him as though He were a distant and selfish tyrant, insensible to His children's cry. It is a mother heart to whom we speak, and one who is always within whispering distance of her little ones.

Let us nestle beneath her wings, let us walk in the light of her love, let us trust the Holy Ghost with implicit, childlike confidence, and always expect the answering voice and presence of the Comforter, and it shall be true, "Before they call I will answer, while they are yet speaking I will hear." The apostle asks the Galatians, "Received ye the Spirit by the works of the law, or by the hearing of faith?" and adds after, "we might receive the promise of the Spirit through faith."

This is the only way that we can receive a person -- by treating him with confidence, believing that he comes to us in sincerity, and opening the door to him at once, recognize him as a friend, and treat him as a welcome guest. So let us treat the Holy Spirit.

4. Let us obey the Spirit.

The first thing in obedience is to hearken. Especially is this necessary with the gentle Comforter. So gentle is this mother that her voice is not often loud, and may be missed by the inattentive ear; therefore, the beautiful expression is used by the apostle Paul in the 8th chapter of Romans, which reminds us of a mother's voice; "The minding of the Spirit is life and peace." We are to mind the Spirit, we are to pay attention to His counsels, commands, and slightest intimations. God never speaks an idle word, nor gives a lesson that we can afford to slight or forget. They who will listen will have much to listen to, but they who slight the voice of God need not wonder that they are often left in silence.

The Spirit's voice is "a still small voice." The heart in which He loves to dwell is a quiet one, where the voice of passion and the world's loud tumult is stilled, and His whisper is watched for with delight and attention.

But not only must we hearken; when we know we must obey. The voice of the Spirit is imperative; there can be no compromise, and there should be no delay. God will not excuse us from His commandments. His word is very deliberately spoken and for our good always, and when the command is given it cannot be recalled. Therefore, if we do not obey we must be involved in darkness, difficulty, and separation from Him. We may plunge on, but the Spirit waits at that point, on the crossroads of life, and we can make no progress until we return and obey Him. Many a bitter experience, many a tear of brokenhearted disappointment and failure have come from refusing to obey. Indeed, such disobedience must be fatal if persisted in. It was just there that Saul halted and lost his kingdom, through disobedience and willfulness in neglecting the voice of God. It was there that Israel found the fatal crisis of their history at Kadesh Barnea. It was there that, in the apostolic days, a nation was about to reap the same fatal error, and the apostle pleaded with his countrymen so solemnly and gently: "Today if ye will hear His voice harden not your hearts."

Happy the heart that promptly obeys the voice of God. The Spirit delights to lead such a soul. How beautifully we see this illustrated in the experience of Paul! At one period of his ministry he was in danger of pressing on in his work beyond the divine command, and so, we are told, he was forbidden of the Spirit to preach the Word in Asia, and essayed to go into Bithynia but the Spirit suffered him not. Happy for him that he obeyed both these restraints. Had he persisted in his way, and even succeeded in getting down to Ephesus, he would have found every door closed, and his visit would have been premature. Waiting on God's bidding and way a year longer, he was permitted to go afterwards and found the door wide open; and his next and perhaps most successful ministry was given to him at Ephesus, while in obedience, that which led him now into Europe. He was permitted to establish the Gospel in that mighty continent.

A little later, we see the very opposite lesson exemplified in his life. We are told that he purposed in Spirit to go to Jerusalem and Rome. This was a personal direction of the Holy Ghost to him, and in consequence he determined upon the greatest purpose of his life, to carry the gospel to his countrymen at Jerusalem, and then to establish Christianity in the capital of the world.

It was well that he proposed it in the Spirit, and that he was sure of God's command, for the difficulties that afterwards met him would have been insuperable on any human line.

First, the very servants of God met him all along the way, and even prophetic messengers warned him not to go to Jerusalem, but the brave apostle kept to his promise and pressed divinely on.

Next, the whole power of unbelieving Judaism arrayed itself against him, tried to mob him at Jerusalem, to assassinate him on the way to Caesarea, and then to condemn him before the tribunal of Felix, Festus and Agrippa, but still he pressed steadfastly on.

Next, the intriguing policy and imperial power of Rome itself confronted him, and held him two years a prisoner at Caesarea, but he never for a moment abandoned his purpose.

At length he was on his way to Rome, but then the very elements of nature and the powers of hell combined in one last effort to destroy him. The fierce Euroclydon of the Mediterranean wrecked his ship, and on Malta's shore the viper from the flames fastened upon his hand, but he still pressed on in indomitable might, in obedience to the Holy Ghost, and so he reached Rome and planted the standard of the cross before the palace of the Caesars, witnessed for Christ in the face of imprisonment and martyrdom, and at last looked down from heaven on the spectacle of Christianity the established religion of the whole Roman empire three hundred years later.

Thus let us obey the Holy Ghost, whether it be in silence or in activity, and we shall find that if He be to us our Wonderful Counselor, He shall certainly prove our mighty God.

5. Let us honor the Holy Ghost.

Less than any other person does He honor Himself. His constant business is to exalt Christ and hide behind His person. Therefore, the Father is pleased when we exalt and honor Him, and He Himself will especially use the instrument which gives Him the glory. "Honor the Holy Ghost and He will honor you," was the counsel of an aged Christian patriarch who had seen many a mighty awakening in the church of God.

It is indeed true and especially important in this material and rationalistic age, when even the ministers of Christ sometimes seem to wish to eliminate the supernatural from the Scriptures and the church, and find any other explanation than the power of God for His supernatural working.

The special dispensation of the Holy Ghost is drawing to its close. We may therefore expect that He will manifest His power in unusual methods and degrees as the age draws to its close.

Let us understand Him and be in sympathy with His divine thought, and ready to follow His wise and mighty leadership unto the last campaign of Christianity. Why should we ever be looking back to Pentecost? Why should we not expect His mightiest triumphs in the immediate future, and, as Joel has prophesied, "before the great and terrible day of the Lord."

Chapter 14: HINDERING THE HOLY SPIRIT.

"Grieve not the Holy Spirit of God." Eph. 4: 30.

"Ye do always resist the Holy Ghost." Acts 7: 51.

"Quench not the Spirit." 1 Thess. 5: 19.

It is very touching and solemn that while the Holy Ghost might, in the exercise of His omnipotence, coerce our will, and compel us to submit to His authority, yet He approaches us with the most deferential regard for our feelings and independence, even suffering us to resist and disobey Him, and bearing long with our willfulness and waywardness.

There are several terms used in the Scriptures to denote the manner in which we may sin against the Holy Spirit.

I. We May Quench the Spirit.

This has reference, perhaps, mainly to the hindrance we offer to His work in others, rather than to our resistance of His personal dealings with our own souls.

Among the various hindrances which we may offer to the Holy Spirit may be mentioned such as these:

1. We may refuse to obey His impulses in us when He bids us speak or act for Him. We may be conscious of a distinct impression of the Spirit of God bidding us to testify for Christ, and by disobedience, or timidity, or procrastination, we may quench His working, both in our own soul and in the heart of another.

2. We may suppress His voice in others, either by using our authority to restrain His messages, when He speaks through His servants or refusing to allow the liberty of testimony. Many hold the reins of ecclesiastical authority unduly, and thus lose the free and effectual working of the Holy Ghost in their churches and in their work.

There is a less direct way, however, of politely silencing Him by forcing Him out, and so filling the atmosphere with the spirit of stiffness, criticism, and a certain air of respectability and rigidness that He gently withdraws from the uncongenial scene, and refuses to thrust His messages upon unwilling hearts.

3. The Spirit may be grieved by the method of public worship in a congregation.

It may be either so stiff and formal that there is no room for His spontaneous working, or so full of worldly and unscriptural elements as to repel and offend Him from taking any part in a pompous ritual. An operatic choir and a ritualistic service will effectually quench all the fire of

God's altar, and send the gentle dove to seek a simpler nest.

4. The Spirit may be quenched by the preacher, and his spirit and method.

His own manner may be so intellectual and self-conscious, and his own spirit so thoroughly cold and vain that the Holy Ghost is neither recognized nor known in his work. His sermons may be on themes in which the Spirit has no interest, for He only witnesses to the Holy Scriptures and the person of Christ, and wearily turns away from the discussion of philosophy, and the stale show of critical brilliancy over the questions of the day or the speculations of man's own vain reason.

Perhaps his address is so rigidly written down that the Holy Spirit could not find an opportunity for even a suggestion, if He so desired, and His promptings and leading so coolly set aside by a course of elaborate preparation which leaves no room for God.

5. The spirit of error in the teachings of the pulpit will always quench the Holy Spirit.

He is jealous for His own inspired Word and when vain man attempts to set it aside He looks on with indignation, and exposes such teachers to humiliation and failure.

The spirit of self-assertion and self -consciousness is always fatal to the free working of the Holy Ghost.

When a man stands up in the sacred desk to air his eloquence and call attention to his intellectual brilliancy, or to preach himself in any sense, he will always be deserted by the Holy Spirit. He uses the things "that are not to bring to naught the things that are." And before we can expect to become the instruments of His power, we must wholly cease from self and be lost in the person and glory of Jesus.

6. The spirit of pride, fashion and worldly display in the pews, is just as fatal as ambition in the pulpit.

Such an atmosphere seems to freeze out the spirit of devotion, and erect on the throne of the lowly Nazarene a goddess of carnal pride and pleasure, like the foul Venus that the Parisian mob set up in the Madeleine at Paris in the days of the revolution, as an object of worship. From such an atmosphere the Holy Ghost turns away grieved and disgusted.

7. The quickening and reviving influences of the Holy Ghost are often quenched in the very hour of promise by wrong methods in the work of Christ's church.

How often, on the eve of a real revival, the minds of the people have been led away by some public entertainment in connection with the house of God, or its after-fruits withered by a series of unholy fairs and secular bids for money, and the introduction of the broker and the cattle-vender into the cleansed temple of Jehovah, as in the days of Christ.

8. The spirit of criticism and controversy is fatal to the working of the Holy Ghost.

The gentle dove will not remain in an atmosphere of strife. If we would cherish His power we must possess His love, and frown down all wrangling gossip, evil speaking, malice, envy, and public controversy in the preaching of the Word.

Sometimes a single word of criticism after an impressive service will dispel all its blessed influence upon the heart of some interested hearer, and counteract the gracious work that would have resulted in the salvation of the soul.

A frivolous Christian woman returning one night from church with her unsaved husband, was laughing lightly at some of the mistakes and eccentricities of the speaker. Suddenly she felt his arm trembling; she looked in his face and his tears were falling. He gently turned to her, and said: "Pray for me; I have seen myself tonight as I never did before." She suddenly awoke with an awful shudder to realize that she had been frivolously wrecking his soul's salvation, and quenching the Holy Ghost.

And so, public controversy is as fatal to the Spirit's working as personal criticism.

It is when the children of God unite at the feet of Jesus, and together seek His blessing, that He comes in all the fullness of His life-power.

At the Council of Nice it is said that a great number of grievances were sent unto Constantine, the presiding officer. After the opening of the great Council, he ordered them to be gathered into the center of the large hall, and then a fire kindled under them, and as they went up in smoke and flame, the Spirit of God fell upon the assembled multitude, and they all felt that in the burning of their strifes and selfish grievances they had received the very baptism of the Holy Ghost.

The Spirit may be quenched in the hearts of our friends by unwise counsel, or ungodly influence.

The little child may be discouraged from seeking Christ by a worldly parent, or the ignorant assumption that it is too young to be a Christian, or too busy with its studies, or its social enjoyments, for such things.

The attractions of the world and claims and pressures of business, may be interposed in the way of some seeking heart, and we find in eternity that we put a stumbling-block in our friend's way, from which he fell into perdition.

Let us be very careful lest, in our willfulness and pride, we not only miss ourselves the inner chambers of the kingdom of heaven, but hinder those that would enter from going in.

Oh! if we would cherish the faintest breath of life in the rescued waif that has been snatched from a watery grave, if we could fan the expiring flame of life in a friend's bosom, let us be careful lest we quench the spark of everlasting life in a human soul, and stand at the last, responsible for the murder of immortal beings, and crimson with the blood of souls. "Quench not the Spirit."

II. We May Grieve the Spirit.

This is a very tender expression; it suggests His gentleness and patience; grieved rather than angry with His unfaithful and distrustful children.

1. We may grieve Him by our doubts and distrust of His love and promises. Thus Moses grieved Him when he struck the rock instead of gently speaking.

Many are afraid of the Holy Ghost and think Him a despot and a terror; shrinking even from His too close approach, as though He would consume us by His holiness. He wants us to love Him, and come near to Him as the gentle mother; to believe in His promises, to count Him faithful, and to treat Him as one who does come to us and dwell within us.

2. We grieve the Holy Spirit when we refuse to wholly yield ourselves to Him, and hold back from entire abandonment and surrender, or when, having so surrendered ourselves, we shrink back from His actual leading and refuse to meet the tests He brings, and lie upon the wheel in stillness while He molds the plaster in clay.

He is grieved at our willfulness and rebellion and resistance. He knows we are losing a blessing, and that we must again go through the same discipline if we are to have our blessings from Him.

He sees in it the spirit of distrust and unbelief, and He feels wounded and slighted by our shrinking.

3. We grieve the Holy Spirit when we fail to enter into the fullness of His grace, and receive the Lord Jesus Christ as our complete Savior.

He has not written one word that we can afford to allow to become of none effect. It is an insult to His wisdom and love to treat the higher visions of His grace as if they were not binding upon our life.

They should fully honor Him, press forward into all His will, and feel they owe to Him as well as themselves that they should lose nothing of all that He has wrought, nor seem to come short of entering into His rest.

Oh, how many of His children are grieving Him as a mother would be grieved, if after having, at great cost and toil, provided bountifully for her children, they should refuse her bounty or despise her rich provision!

4. We grieve the Holy Spirit when we fail to hearken to His voice.

He is constantly calling upon us to listen, and He never speaks in vain, nor can we ever afford to miss the slightest whisper. When, therefore, we fail to hearken, and dash along with heedless impulsiveness, He is deeply grieved, and has to call in the loud and painful tones of trial and chastening.

How He bewails His ancient people for their refusing to listen to His living voice: "Oh, that my people had hearkened to my commandments, then had their peace been like a river, and their righteousness as the waves of the sea."

5. We grieve the Holy Spirit when, having heard, we presume to disobey His voice.

This is very serious, and full of terrible danger. It is an awful thing willfully to neglect or defy the distinct command of the Holy Ghost. We cannot do it without losing the sense of His presence, and being conscious that He has withdrawn the manifestation of His love, until we deeply and penitently recognize our sin, and step into the path of obedience where we separated from His companionship.

6. Nothing grieves the Holy Spirit more than a divided heart and the cherishing of any idols in our affections which separate our supreme love from Christ.

There is a remarkable passage in the book of James which declares that "the Spirit which dwelleth in us loveth us to jealousy" (marginal reading), and in the same connection it is added, "Ye adulterers and adulteresses, know ye not that the friendship of the world is enmity with God?" that is, a heart set upon earthly things is guilty of spiritual adultery, the Holy Ghost looks upon it with jealous love, grieved and insulted by the dishonor done to our divine husband by our unfaithful affections.

7. We grieve the Holy Spirit whenever we neglect, pervert, or dishonor the Holy Scriptures.

This is His word, and not one utterance or one jot shall fall to the ground. How we grieve Him when we explain its precious promises, and make of none effect its exact commands; and how He loves the heart that feeds upon the truth and honors the Bible in its least promise and command!

8. Especially do we grieve the Holy Ghost when we dishonor Jesus, or let anything separate us from Him, or cloud our conception of Him, and interrupt our devotion to Him.

He is jealous for the honor of Christ; therefore, whenever self, or any human being comes between us and Christ, whenever the glory of the Master is obscured by the glory of the servant, whenever even truth or work becomes more distinct than Christ Himself, the Holy Ghost is grieved; and He is pleased when we exalt the Savior, and give Him all the glory.

9. The Holy Spirit is grieved when we ignore Him.

He longs after our love and trust.

10. The Holy Spirit is especially grieved by a spirit of bitterness toward any human being, and therefore the apostle says, "Let all bitterness, and wrath, and anger, and clamor, and evil speaking be put away from you with all malice. And grieve not the Holy Spirit of God, whereby we are sealed unto the day of redemption."

III. We May Resist the Holy Spirit.

This has special reference to the attitude of the unbeliever, with whom the Holy Ghost is striving with a view to convict him of sin and lead Him to the Savior.

1. The sinner resists the Holy Spirit when he tries to shake off religious impressions.

This may be done in many ways. Sometimes the soul, under the Spirit's striving, tries to quench its impressions in pleasure, excitement or business. Sometimes it treats them as nervous depression, low spirits or ill-health, and seeks a remedy in change of scene or thought; very often it resorts to light reading, worldly amusements, frivolous society, perhaps indulgence in sin, and the devil always has plenty of auxiliaries to suggest distracting thoughts, and help to dispel the sacred influences that God is gathering around the heart.

Very often it will become provoked and offended with some acts on the part of Christians, sometimes perhaps connected with the religious services, and will resolve to give up attending, or find some petty excuse for getting out of the way of the influences that are troubling its contentment. All these efforts to escape are but the stronger evidence of the Spirit's striving, and He patiently and lovingly continues to press the arrow still more keenly into the wounded heart, until it is laid prostrate at the feet of love.

2. The sinner resists the influences of the Holy Spirit in leading him to conviction of sin.

It is not enough to awaken concern in the soul, and even alarm -- there must be a distinct working of Scriptural conviction in order to secure lasting peace and sound conversion; and, therefore, the Holy Ghost has promised to convict the world of sin.

He does this by bringing before the conscience the memory of actual transgressions -- the recollection of any forgotten sins, the iniquities of youth and childhood, the secret sins known to God only, the aggravations of sin, the warnings and light against which it has been committed, the love that has been resisted, the threatenings of the divine law, the unchangeable holiness of the divine character, the tremendous sentence against all iniquity, the deep inward consciousness of guilt, the still more terrible sense of the wickedness of the sinner's heart, the hopeless depravity, the consciousness of willfulness and unbelief, and the dreadful fear of its hopelessness, the impossibility of its salvation.

Thus the Great Advocate sets in array our transgressions, until the heart seeks some escape from itself, and Satan is ready to suggest a thousand excuses, palliations and false hopes, through which the guilty spirit seeks to evade the force of its conviction.

It thinks of the faults of others, and plausible reasons that it is no worse than they; it eagerly seizes upon the inconsistencies of Christians, and tries to excuse itself by their failure; it recalls its own miserable attempts at goodness, and tries to find some comfort in its own righteousness; it seeks false refuge in the mercy of God, and eagerly tries to persuade itself that the picture of Christ's anger against sin, and the stories of judgment and perdition, are fictions of obsolete theology.

It says peace, peace, when there is no peace, and heals slightly its hurt, resisting with all its might the blessed Spirit, who wounds only that He may heal.

Happy they who fail in the foolish attempt, and in whose hearts the arrows of the King are so sharp and keen that the wound can never be stanched save by the blood of Calvary.

3. The sinner resists the work of the Holy Ghost in leading him to decision.

Even after he has been driven from his previous refuges, and has been awakened to his profound concern, and thoroughly convicted of his sin, and fully admits the claims of religion and the justness of his condemnation, he seeks another door of escape in procrastination.

He will surrender, he will resist no more, he will accept the Savior, but not now, he is not quite ready yet.

Perhaps he argues that he does not feel strongly enough, that he wants a deeper conviction, more light, a little more deliberate consideration, perhaps a little more time to alter his circumstances and change his life; but really what he is pleading for is a reprieve for his sinful heart, a little longer in the indulgence of his self-will, and disobedience to the gospel.

And his course is just as dangerous and just as truly a rejection of Christ as if he did it deliberately and directly; while at the same time it has the self-deceiving aspect of being a sort of yielding, at least a nominal consent, to all the pleadings of the Holy Ghost. He is resisting the Spirit, and his tomorrow often means, as the eyes of heaven read the words, NEVER.

4. The sinner resists the Holy Spirit in His gracious attempts to convict the soul of righteousness and lead it to believe on the Son of God.

The Spirit's object is not merely to produce concern, alarm, and even the profoundest repentance, but the blessed goal of all His gracious movements is the trustful acceptance of Jesus, and the believing assurance of His forgiveness and salvation.

It is here that Satan and self-will fight their hardest battle. The soul will consent to live a better life, will be willing to weep and mourn, will do anything rather than accept the very gift of salvation and believe the naked word of God, that its sins are forgiven for His name's sake, and that it is accepted in Jesus Christ, as He is accepted.

How desperately it fights against this simple act, clothing its unbelief in the guise of humanity and modesty, and thinking it presumption to dare to make such a claim!

Many souls hold back at this point for months and years, and know not that in all their doubts and fears, their hard thoughts of themselves and of God, they are simply resisting the Holy Ghost, who is striving with them to lay their sins forever at the feet of Jesus, and go forth into His everlasting peace.

5. At this point the resisting soul is led by this great enemy to erect a whole line of false refuges, and run under their cover, instead of fleeing for refuge directly to the hope set before it in the gospel.

One of these refuges is outward reformation of life. The sinner will do better, will take the pledge, will turn over a new leaf, will make large promises and comfort his soul with the flattering unction that he is a changed man, while all the while he has the same evil heart, and it will produce the same fruits when the mere effort of will has spent itself.

Another refuge of lies is a religious profession. He will get confirmed or join the church and begin a life of formalism; perhaps give something to the cause of Christ, and even attempt some Christian work, but he is only a whitewashed Pharisee, and within the sepulcher are dead men's bones and all uncleanliness; and he will find before long, that his old heart has still the same loves and hates, yet he has effectually suppressed the voice of the Spirit.

He meets every fear and conviction with the consciousness of his religious profession, and he will even go to the gates of the judgment hall saying, "Have we not eaten and drunken in Thy presence! and Thou hast taught in our streets;" but He will profess unto them, "I never knew you."

Poor Ignorance, in Pilgrim's Progress, went up to the very gates of heaven with an easy conscience; every conviction had been stifled by his shallow professions and imagined works of self-righteousness; and so multitudes have escaped the pain of an evil conscience, and the Spirit's striving, to find it turn in the hour of judgment into the remorseful horror of eternal condemnation.

And so we might speak of almost countless other false refuges, all of which have the effect of quieting the troubled heart, but not saving the soul. They are like sandbags thrown up in the outworks of our souls, in which the arrows of the Lord are lost or muffled, but which are no protection from the armies of destruction.

6. It is possible for the soul to resist the Holy Ghost openly, directly, willfully, and presumptuously, until it drives Him from its door and commits the fatal sin of willfully rejecting the offered Savior in the full light of the Holy Spirit's revealing, and perhaps with the full consciousness that it is defiantly refusing God.

There is such a thing referred to in the Scriptures, "If ye refuse and rebel ye shall be destroyed;" "I called and ye refused." "If we sin willfully after that we have received the knowledge of the truth, there remaineth no more sacrifice for sins, but a certain fearful looking for of judgment and fiery indignation, which shall devour the adversaries. He that despised Moses' law died without mercy under two or three witnesses. Of how much sorer punishment, suppose ye, shall he be thought worthy who hath trodden under foot the Son of God, and hath counted the blood of the covenant, wherewith he was sanctified, an unholy thing, and hath done despite unto the Spirit of grace? For we know Him that hath said, Vengeance belongeth unto me, I will recompense, saith the Lord. And again, The Lord shall judge His people. It is a fearful thing to fall into the hands of the living God."

The blasphemy of the Pharisees against the Holy Ghost seems to have consisted in rejecting Jesus after they had sufficient light to know that He was the Son of God.

It was, therefore, not only the rejection of Jesus, but the deliberate rejection of the Holy Ghost and His witness to Jesus, when they knew it to be His witness.

Essentially, therefore, it is the same sin as any soul may now commit, when in the full light of God, and conscious that He has directly called it to accept the Savior, it defiantly refuses.

The effect of such an act may be, and perhaps usually is, the withdrawal of the Spirit from the soul until it is left, past feeling, to a hardened heart, and a doom on which the voice of divine appeal and the light of mercy will never fall again.

This is, perhaps, what is meant by the blasphemy against the Holy Ghost which never hath forgiveness.

Let no one think he has committed this sin if still in the heart there is a willingness to yield to God and accept the Savior.

If there is even a fear that any reader may have committed this sin, and a great longing that it may not be so, rejoice exceedingly, and yield this moment even to His faint touch of heavenly influence, lest it should be withdrawn, and the soul left under the sad sentence, "He is joined to his idols, let him alone." The good Payson once said to his young friend, who had spoken of a slight religious influence, and wondered if it was enough to act upon, "A little cord has dropped from heaven, so fine that you can scarcely feel it or perceive it; it just touches your shoulder for a moment; dear friend, grasp it quickly, for it fastens to the throne of God, and it is for you perhaps the last strand of saving mercy; grasp it and never let it go, and it will grow into a cable of strength that will anchor you to the skies and keep your precious soul unto everlasting life."

Oh! let us be fearful and careful lest we sin against the Holy Ghost by quenching the Spirit, by grieving the Holy One, by resisting our best Friend, or by blaspheming His mighty name.

Made in the USA
Las Vegas, NV
04 October 2022

56549678R00046